MW00961060

On The Shoulders
of Giants

Contemplating the Super Scientific
On My Journey Towards Enlightenment

By:
Philip M. Kava

Forward
By:
Dr. R. Leo Sprinkle

Copyright © 2013 by Philip M. Kava

All rights reserved. No part of this book may be reproduced or
transmitted in any form or by any means, electronic or mechanical,
including photocopying, recording, or by any information storage and
retrieval system, without permission in writing from publisher.

Published and cover design by Philip M. Kava, Stanton Michigan.

Distributed by Amazon Publishing

ISBN-13: 978-1494790042

Dedications

I want to dedicate this book to my wife Holly and all of our children and grandchildren.

To Ashley, Philip, Eden, Chris, Tracy, Mathew, and Alexandria, and all the grandchildren; With all of my love, I give these words to you so that one day you may read them and understand how I became who I am; and what I truly believe.

To Holly, Thank you for believing in me. Maybe this will help truly answer the one question you have asked me a million times; "What are you thinking about?" Well this is what I've been thinking about.

Special Thank You to:
Dr. R. Leo Sprinkle
and
Alex Dimitrijevic

"If I have seen a little further it is by standing on the shoulders of Giants."

Sir Isaac Newton 1676

In Memory Of:

Lefty Levengood

1925-2013

My friend and mentor,
His journey has just begun.

Preface

I started to write this book in 2003 and again in 2011. In January 2013 I saw, what appeared to be, a Grey Alien hovering over my wife, as we lied in bed. After that event I decided the time had come to finish this project. I am a long time ET experiencer, and I have some stories of life changing experiences I would like to share with you; in hopes that they may help you better understand this multidimensional reality; in which, we currently reside.

Over the past fifteen years or longer I have had dozens, perhaps hundreds of daytime U.F.O. sightings; many of them with multiple witnesses. In fact, my multiple experiences with ET's were interesting enough to grab the attention of a documentary film crew from the U.K. So, in April, 2013 I became a contributor to a U.F.O. Documentary; which is supposed to be part of a new television series on a major U.S. cable television network. Due to the legalities involved with the nondisclosure contract I signed; I can't name the production company or the major U.S. cable network the show will air on, at this point in time.

Allow me to explain why I agreed to tell my story to millions of television viewers around the world. I have lived a life of persistent and perpetual weirdness, and countless miracles. Since my early childhood I have had lucid flying dreams, out of body experiences, precognitive dreams, spirit guide or angelic contact, contact with extraterrestrial or multi-dimensional beings, multiple U.F.O. sightings and have witnessed apparition type miracles related to the Mother Mary. '*In August, 1996 myself along with a couple of hundred other people witnessed a white concrete, life sized, statue of the Mother Mary, holding the baby Jesus; form dark pupils in the eyes and then her whole face smiled.*'

Finally there is the previously mentioned, Grey hovering over my bed. This lifetime of strange events has kept me on the search for answers since these things began to occur to me. So, one of the reasons I agreed to contribute to the television program was, to try to help all of us find answers to some of these bazaar events which have occurred in my life. I am hoping that some of the details I shared with the investigators involved with T.V. program, will help U.F.O. investigators worldwide uncover more answers about extraterrestrial and inter-dimensional beings.

There is another reason I agreed to participate in the T.V. program; it has to do with the scientific research I have been involved with for over 13 years. For over 30 years I have been investigating and dabbling with energy healing, subtle energy and energy medicine. Beginning in 2000-2001 I started participating in research with biophysicist W.C. Levengood. To his friends he is known as Lefty; and that is how I will refer to him. In the mid to late 1990's, Lefty and Dr. John L. Gedye developed and patented, "the CDP device", a device which measures subtle energies in living organisms. To put it simply; they developed a device and methodology to measure a humans bio-intrinsic energy fields, or their chi.

For over 10 years I have repeatedly conducted experiments using the CDP device, which can scientifically prove that human beings can use the intent of their minds to send bio-intrinsic energies to other people from a few feet away or over great distances. I have been aware of this technology for years and I thought that if I agreed to participate in the T.V. show I may get to talk about the CDP device with the show's producers; possibly getting the opportunity to share it with the viewers of the program.

Unfortunately, there was another, more personal reason I wanted the world to find out about the CDP device as soon as possible. You see, just prior to being asked to do the T.V. show, Lefty became very ill; and was forced to be admitted to a long term rehabilitation facility. I hoped we could get some publicity on the CDP device before he was gone. Although the CDP device has been patented for nearly twenty years; and the developers have published scientific papers on the data in reputable publications; very few people are aware of the CDP device and what we can measure with it. Well, the producers did not include any discussion on the CDP device on the T.V. show, but I did get a chance share the technology with the show's producers.

Now let me tell you what happened during the filming of the T.V. show. During the many meetings I had with the T.V. show's producers, I did spark their interest in the CDP device and what research conducted with it has shown. They wanted to speak with Lefty, but he was in no shape to conduct another television interview. In an effort to give the best demonstration of the CDP device I could, I needed a really good energy worker. So I contacted Edd, a medical intuitive with very good control of his bio-intrinsic energy fields and the ability to manipulate the bio-intrinsic energy fields of others. Edd has the ability to send energies across great distances with ease. Edd can use the intent of his mind and the power of his brain to physically move crowds of people. Edd can do other astonishing things as well.

Edd came to my home for the filming of the T.V. show and met with the producers, he gave each one of them a personal demonstration of his abilities. After careful observation of Edd physically moving people with the power of his mind from ten feet away; I figured out how he does it. What is even cooler than that is that I am going to tell you how it is done. I believe there is a good chance you will be able to do it. This is just one example of the answers I have in store for you within the content of this book.

Forward
By:
Dr. R. Leo Sprinkle

It is a pleasure to write these comments for Phil Kava and his book. Like many other writers, who now are describing their experiences with Star People, or Extra Terrestrials (ETs), Phil is sharing what he knows with his readers. These writers may not view themselves as accomplished authors, but they know that they are, not only telling their stories; they also are serving as messengers to humanity.

Some researchers have presented various scenarios about the ET presence and their possible motives:

- Invaders? (E.g.; Dr. David Jacobs, PhD).
- Intruders? (E.g.: Budd Hopkins, n.d.).
- Instructors? (E.g.; Dr. Ken Ring, PhD).
- Initiators? (E.g.: Dr. Jim Deardorff, PhD).

In this latter scenario, ETs present themselves-not as themselves, but as "mirrors" of who we are, and what we fear or hope, or seek, etc.

Paola Harris has interviewed Vatican officials, Rev. Balducci and Dr. Funes, who view ETs-not as Angels or Devils, but as Brothers and Sisters of the Cosmos.

Many researchers have sought to expose the U.F.O. Cover up, seeking ways to encourage governmental officials to release information about their U.F.O. reports. Many nations have released data, but the "Big Three" (China, Russia, and the U.S.A.) have yet to do so. Soon?

More and more researchers are concluding that the "true" secret is not the ET presence. It is the availability of energy technologies. For example, Nicola Tesla, in his struggle with Thomas Edison about direct current (DC) versus alternating current (AC), was investigating the possibility of sending electricity by land or by air.

Dr. Tom Valone, PhD, and others are writing about ZPE (Zero Point Energy) and many other sources and systems of non- polluting energy. If the true secret of the U.F.O. conveys the availability of energy technologies, then the important question becomes:

Can we humans learn to control our greed and our violence, and can we share "free energy" with everyone on the planet?

If so, there would be no need for us humans to rape Mother Earth for oil, gas, coal; no need for nuclear fission; and no need for war between who are competing for soil, oil, water, and air.

As Dolan and Zabel have stated in their book, AD After Disclosure, the announcement of the ET presence is both "inevitable and imminent." When the Breakaway Group, or the Secret Keepers, decide to disclose the ET presence-and the energy technologies-and then Humanity enters into a Golden

Age of Synthesis: Masculine and Feminine; Science and Spirit; Technology and Humanism. Sharing and serving all (not only humans and ETs, but Mother Earth and Her Denizens).

I am pleased that Phil Kava is willing to share his experiences and insights, with us. May his message be given, far and wide, and may we all share.

Love and Light

R. Leo Sprinkle, PhD.
Professor Emeritus,
University of Wyoming

Love and Light,
Leo

Table of Contents

Introduction

Have you ever wondered who you are and why you're here, have you ever pondered the existence of alien beings from distant worlds or other dimension? Are we being visited by these beings? Have you ever wondered what it would take to make something invisible? Have you ever thought it may be possible to heal yourself, others, or the planet, with nothing more than a touch, a prayer, or a thought? If you have answered yes to any of these questions, you are not alone, so please continue.

Within the chapters of this book I present some stories of my journey toward enlightenment. I will discuss my views on some of the topics I have been researching for over 30 years. I will discuss everything from Consciousness, Energy Healing, Extraterrestrials, Multiple Dimensions, Subtle Energies, the Power of Intent, Quantum Physics, Quantum Mechanics, Reality, Our Potential Future and much more. I hope the personal experiences I share and my views of reality, will help you to expand your understanding of what and who you really are, what you are capable of and how, together, we create our reality.

Chapter 1
Growing Up in the Late Seventies

I will start at a relative starting point, my grandparents. All of my grandparents were coal miners and moonshiners. They raised my parents in the foothills of the Appalachian Mountains in central Pennsylvania. My Mom's mother died when my mom was only four years old. My mom's father died when she was nine. She was adopted and raised by a large family that lived down the street from her. My dad's parents lived a much longer life in comparison. My dad's father died in October 1965. I found out a few years back that out of the eleven children my parents had I was the only planned birth. My mom told me I was conceived shortly after my grandfather's death. I was born in July 1966. My dad's mother, Grandma Kava, always called me her little angel. I always pondered that term of endearment. It was not until I was nineteen that I found out that my grandfather was a "faith healer." That was very significant to me and I will explain in detail later.

My parents married in 1947 when my dad returned from the South Pacific after World War II. They went to Michigan for their honeymoon and ended up staying. They raised eleven children in the suburbs west of Detroit, on a mechanic's salary. They did the best they could; but when I hit my pre-teen years in the late seventies, they were worn out and tired of parenting. They lost all control over me by the time I was twelve and I pretty much did what I wanted, when I wanted.

I can't remember the first time I smoked marijuana, not because I was too stoned, it's because I was only four years old. Apparently my eldest brother needed a smoking buddy and I was elected. I didn't start using drugs on my own until I was twelve. I was born and raised in the suburbs about twenty miles southwest of Detroit. I rarely had to buy pot because my brothers and sisters would give it to me.

The first day of eighth grade I skipped school, dropped three hits of orange micro-dot mescaline and watched merry-go-rounds in the sky. I was kicked out of eighth grade two weeks early for creating a disturbance in the lunch room. I saw it as an early summer vacation.

I returned to high school for the first few months of ninth grade. At that time I could get a nice big ounce of pot for $35, roll a hundred joints out of it and sell them for a dollar a piece before school started. I was an entrepreneur even back then. The first day of tenth grade I was invited to the principal's office and asked if I would like to quit school. So I signed papers, stating the school and I agreed that I did not need to attend school. So at fifteen I was free to go and off I went.

Allow me to regress to a time prior to my running wild; when I was eleven years old. Some of these events were very influential in determining who I would become. My grandmother, the one which called me her little angel, died a couple of days after Christmas 1977. Fortunately we had gone to spend that Christmas with her in Pennslyvania. She had been ill for some time, but refused to go to the doctors. She believed in faith healing and had never seen a doctor. I think she was seventy-seven at the time. I asked her to please go to the doctor, so she did. Grandma always said, "Never tell someone goodbye, always say, see you later." Well as they left the house I said, "Goodbye, Grandma." As the car drove off, I remembered what she had always said and ran outside to say, "See you later," but it was too late. They had already left. I never saw her again. She died later that night.

About six months later, death had again struck very close to home. By mid June 1978, two friends of the family, my sister's boyfriend, Jeff, and my brother's friend, Brian, were both killed in separate motorcycle accidents. About two weeks before Jeff died, he had quit school. One day, shortly after Jeff quit, for some reason, I was hiding beneath one of the end tables in our living room when he and my sister entered the room. My sister was trying to convince him to return to school and this was his response. "I'm seventeen years old and haven't done shit with my life. I want to live a little before I'm dead, I could die tomorrow and what do I have to show for myself? I've wasted enough time in school."

A couple of weeks later I was in our front yard playing Frisbee with my stoner brother, when my brother's friend Brian pulled up on his new motorcycle. He had just graduated high school and was on his way for a bike trip to the Upper Peninsula. "I finally finished with the bullshit." "No more school," he said to my brother. That was the last time I saw Brian. He was hit by a drunk driver on his way home from his road trip. Jeff died three days before Brian, only two miles from our house. I just did not understand why.

I believe I was eleven maybe only ten when my

cynicism toward God and religion began to surface. I'm pretty sure it was before these three deaths impacted my life. Being raised in a Quasi-Catholic family I was expected to do something called "first confession," where I was supposed to confess my sins to a priest. I didn't get it. I remember telling my mother, "If God is this all knowing being, who knows our every thought; why in the hell do I have to tell another man what I've done wrong?" "Why is this *man* closer to God than me?" My mother had no answer, so I quit. I wasn't buying into their dogmatic bullshit. It's not that I didn't want to believe in God; I did, but where was He? If he was somewhere why did so much bad shit happen, especially to me?

I remember one night staying up very late and writing a paper. I called it the "Philosophils." It was pretty impressive for a twelve year old. It was impressive to my college Philosophy instructor. It really blew his mind, when I told him I was only twelve when I wrote it. I am not sure where I put it or even if I still have it, but it went something like this:

The Philosophils

I am not really sure if there is a God or not. If there is, they say He hears our every thought and knows our every action. There is nothing we do in secret that he does not know about. We are all sinners. We all do bad things as well as good. Let's say for instance there is no God. We still have one person who knows everything we've ever done, the good and the bad. That is our Self. As we go through life we can choose to be good or evil. We are the only one who really knows. So lets say for example you have two people one who spends his life doing the right things to the best of his ability, the other don't give a shit about anyone but himself, screwing anyone he can doing whatever he wants with no regard for others. There will come a point in both of their lives when they will have no choice but to face themselves. That will be the time of their death. They say that when we die our life flashes

25

before our eyes. It is at this point when we cannot hide who we were. It is this point in time, even if it only a matter of seconds, that we will face judgment, from ourselves. It is at this point, if only seconds before complete nothingness engulfs us forever, that we decide whether we go to heaven or hell. In that moment before nothingness how do we judge ourselves? For the one who obeyed the laws of his times and followed his religious beliefs these last few seconds he breathes his last sigh of relief, knowing he has done the right things. No regrets, no fears, he has done his best. He is going to Heaven. For the other guy, the evil one, the story is quite different. In his moments before nothingness his life also flashes before his eyes. He cannot hide from the person he was. He realizes his mistakes, he feels his regrets, but he knows it is too late. He can't go back to change things, to say he is sorry. He feels cold and alone. His anguish begins to burn, like the fiery pits of hell as the dark nothingness overtakes him.

Fifteen was a very trying age for me. I impregnated my girlfriend, her mother made her get an abortion. I was kicked out of school, willingly. I had a large family who did very little to help set me straight. And I had a group of friends that were almost as screwed up as I was. I was very alone and very close to suicide.

Shortly after my girlfriend had her abortion a rather strange event took place. It was an event that didn't make a whole lot of sense until years later. I was a high school drop/kick out, doing any kind of odd job I could to make a few bucks, including selling dope. One day, I was leaving a friend's house a shortly after my girlfriend had her abortion, when this other kid I knew stopped me and asked if I wanted to buy some speed. So I did. I took one hit, or pill. Taking one little amphetamine for me was nothing. I used to take drugs by the hand full and still attend school and get A's and B's, no problem. But this day something happened.

About an hour after I took the speed I went home and started lifting weights. I need to mention that several weeks prior to this day I had begun praying daily. My prayer went something like this, "God, if you are there, please give me a sign, I need to know there is more to life." Well that day, my prayer was answered. I was lifting weights like a mad man and I was on my umpteenth set of bench presses when suddenly it happened. Words cannot fully describe what I saw. It was as if I were suddenly standing on the ground looking up into the sky. But I was actually lying on my weight bench looking at the ceiling. It was as if the ceiling suddenly opened and I saw up into the clouds. There I saw the most beautiful vision. It was Jesus on the cross with an angel on each side of him and immersed in the clouds behind all of them was God with his arms outstretched encompassing the earth. I flipped out. It scared the hell out of me. I thought I had surely died. I jumped up, my heart pounding in my chest I ran upstairs and didn't go in my basement for about three days. I asked for a sign and I got it. Wow. What a trip. Was it an LSD flashback? Maybe it was. But the only one I ever had. Was it a near death experience from a heart attack? Maybe it was. Or was it a sign from God? Although this was not the first super scientific event to occur in my life, it was the most vivid, to that point.

You see as far back as I can remember having dreams, I can remember having dreams that come true. Most of the dreams I have had that come true are of no significance to anyone but me. The first one I remember happened to me in third grade. It was about a certain boy getting chased by a certain girl and the boy fell, got a bloody nose and ran up to me and asked if it was bleeding. It came true the following day. These dreams have haunted me my entire life. They can be very scary at times; especially the dreams I have had of future of mankind.

I have also had out of body experiences and

lucid flying dreams since I was a small child. I want to share one very memorable lucid flying dream I had when I was about eleven years old. One night during the Spring of 1977, while sleeping in my basement bedroom, I left my body and flew out the small basement window to go hunting rabbits. I left our yard and flew to a small patch of woods where we trained our hunting dog. I remember swooping down at a rabbit hiding in a brush pile and making it run off. I followed the rabbit for a minute and then flew back toward my home. I was traveling about 30 feet above the ground, about the height of the power lines. When I came close to the power lines in our backyard, I was stopped by the energy field emitting from the power lines. I began to panic and then realized the power lines were the problem. So I flew away from the power lines and then flew closer to the ground. This allowed me to get past the power lines and fly back into my bedroom and into my body.

When I was sixteen, my life was super

scientifically uneventful. I moved up north to work on a farm and remodel houses. I lived in the sticks for about six months then returned to the Detroit area. My life still sucked. I still felt very alone and was very much without direction.

My life took an adventurous change for the better in November 1983. One of my sisters was moving home from the Naval Base in Guam. Her new fiancé was stationed on the west coast and was soon to depart on a west pack, that's a six month tour in the Pacific. Since my sister was a couple months pregnant and already had two small children, she needed some help settling in to their new home in California. So my brother-in-law to be invited me out to California. November 17, 1983, I took my first plane ride to California.

Chapter 2
Life in the Fast Lane

When opportunity knocks, open the door. This has always been my motto. Life is too short to wait around for it to happen to you. California was a great learning experience for me. After the culture shock wore off, I seemed to fit right in. I started out doing very well. I found a job building furniture in Santee, only a few miles from my apartment in El Cajon. I stayed off all the drugs for at least four months. I worked hard and was promoted to delivery driver. After living in California only a couple of months, I found myself making daily deliveries from San Diego to Bakersfield.

It wasn't long after, I started hanging out with the guys from work who all smoked pot, soon I was back to partying on a daily basis. In a couple of months, my foreman approached me with some Crystal Meth, meth-amphetamines. For a speed freak like me, this was a very dangerous thing.

I had my own apartment and a nice car, a 1970 Ford Mustang fastback, with a built 351. I lived next door to some very busy drug dealers. There was drug traffic all day and night, seven days a week. One day, I was heading out and the neighbor stopped me. He asked me if I wanted to buy some Crystal. "Hell Yeah!" I responded. I soon became good friends with Rob and Deb. Such good friends, in fact, that when they moved a month later they turned the business over to me. I hadn't been in California six months and I was already one of the biggest Meth dealers in El Cajon.

I believe it was early April 1984 when I took over the drug business from my neighbors. Soon after, I quit working. I made enough money selling dope and it took up all of my time. I was only seventeen years old, wild and crazy. I had a new girlfriend every couple of days. I sold dope to the children of multi-millionaires. I associated with junkies and Hell's Angels. I sold dope to people and watched them share dirty needles. I had people go into my bathroom to shoot up Meth in their groin because the veins in their arms were blown out. I've seen people shoot up under their finger nails and in their eyelids, these memories are pretty intense. It has been a long time since I've reflected on those days. I remember all the runaways who stayed at my place from time to time. The thirty-seven year old lady who offered to let me sleep with her and her 17 year old daughter for a few lines of Crystal. The beautiful little girl, age sixteen, who ran up to me in the parking lot of the mall and said, "Aren't you gonna give me a kiss? It's my birthday." I never saw her before in my life. She and her pet tarantula stayed with me for a few weeks.

I learned a lot about life and life's injustices. The one armed homeless guy who was always digging through the dumpster looking for dinner. The shopping cart lady was always walking around in her ragged out clothes. The Vietnamese guy who would scrounge up cans and drove down the road on his moped When you were behind him all you could see was four great big bags of cans and a small tire sticking out from beneath. There was the schizophrenic guy who would hang out at the party store, talking into his shirt collar. He looked like Dusty Roads, the guy from ZZ Top. The little flaming gay guy I worked with who offered to give me the best blow job I ever had, better than any woman could ever do. "Naa, I don't go there." That was nothing new. I've had gay guys hitting on me since I was thirteen. I apologize for leaving out the details of my adventures. They would surely add to the color of this text, but they will have to wait for another book. Besides my kids and grandkids don't need to know everything I've done.

I mentioned earlier how I had often had dreams that came true. Well there was a very specific series of dreams which unfolded in the month prior to my leaving California, which I believe had a life saving message. I remembered having these dreams repeatedly a couple of years before I moved to El Cajon. I really began to flip out my friends when I would tell them as we were going somewhere, whom or what we would see or what was going to happen. To be honest, it was flipping me out as well. Most of the events I predicted were mundane and ordinary things. But I felt something big coming; something very scary. It was one of the nights I almost died.

I was the man with the goods that all the druggies wanted. I sold to ex-cons, bikers, losers and very rich kids. There was one ex-con, loser rich kid in particular who bought a lot of stuff from me every week. His father disowned him and his mother secretly supported him. One day, I gave him a ride to his parent's house in the hills. As we drove up in front of this huge mansion, a helicopter was landing somewhere on the grounds. We stopped at the mailbox and he reached in and pulled out an envelope with ten thousand, in cash, inside. We then proceeded to party. We went to some guy's house and picked up some magic, hallucinogenic, mushrooms. We each ate a few then drove back to his place. We sat around a while bitching about how much life sucked and then the moron had an idea. "Hey," he said, "Lets eat the rest of these shrooms at once." The other two people with us declined the offer, I didn't. He put two hands full of Mushrooms on a Hot Rod magazine and handed it to me. He then took about the same amount and placed them on a magazine in front of himself. We simultaneously, curled up the magazines, placed them to our mouths and tilted our heads back. I had to cram them in my mouth to make them fit. Talk about, nasty it was like eating a cow patty; I suppose.

Twenty minutes later; we were tripping. I had not done hallucinogens in almost three years; this would be the last time. I sat there listening to this spoiled little rich kid and his friends, reality began to sink in. The series of dreams I had years before began to replay right before my eyes. We were all messed up, but the conversation was real, very real. After hours of debating what they all wanted to do with their lives, they came up with an answer. They had decided that all of us would go to Hawaii that night to start a marijuana farm. They were serious and it was very possible, even probable. That is when it hit me. This was the point in my life when I would have to choose between a life of crime or a simpler plan? I stood up and walked out. Being in no condition to drive, I continued to walk, and walk, and walk. I walked until I was lost somewhere downtown, San Diego. At one point, I found myself standing in the middle of highway eight with cars whizzing by me on all sides, honking their horns. Hell, at one point I thought I was a mollusk on the beach. I finally made it to a park bench, it was there I sat and wondered. I sat there long enough to come down. I started to get my bearings straight, and then began my long journey home. On the way, I began to see them: all the homeless people I knew from the neighborhood. I saw the one armed dumpster guy, the shopping cart lady, Dusty, and then the can man. All that night, every minute, everything I saw and heard, I had seen it all before in a dream.

It was a night of revelation. It was a night of remembering. I had often wondered how old someone had to be before they were mature enough to really know right from wrong. I mean, right and wrong from God's perspective. When does God quit saying, "Well, he is just a kid and didn't really know any better, so I will forgive him," for me it was seventeen. You see something strange happened that night. It was like a dream, a memory, may be it was just a hallucination. But at some point that night I found myself in the ether, in the empty space of the universe. I stood in the presence of Christ, next to Him was Lucifer. Looking at me Christ said these words, "Do with him as you wish, for he is my true and faithful servant, and he shall not fail me." No joke, I'm serious.

When I finally made it home the next morning, I went straight into the bathroom and looked in the mirror, it was a pathetic sight. I figure I had probably only slept for a total of two weeks in the past four months. I lost almost thirty pounds and I knew it was do or die. Within two weeks, I sold almost everything I owned, including the Mustang. I bought an old low rider Datsun pickup truck and got the hell outta there. It was time to go home, or so I thought.

Chapter 3
The Longer Journey Home

I packed up everything I had left and a friend who wanted to be dropped off in Arizona, and we hit the road. I made it almost all the way to Phoenix when my truck died. My friend called his sister for a lift to his folks' house. When we finally made it there, his parents said I was welcome to stay. So we both stayed there a few days, then some old friends of his said we could stay with them in Casa Grande. I ended up staying with them a couple of weeks. I soon found a job at the new potato chip factory and moved into my own place. I quit using and stayed clean for the almost seven months I lived there.

While I was there, my strange dreams continued and my "Out of Body Experiences" (OBE) started to become very intense. There was some very heavy spiritual energy in the deserts of Casa Grande. I ended up finding a book at the local library called <u>Journeys Out Of The Body</u> by Robert Monroe. It was quite an eye opener. Instead of fearing these strange occurrences I began to embrace them. I actually got to the point where I could often voluntarily journey out of body while my body was sleeping. Yeah I know it sounds crazy, but stranger things will happen, trust me. There were times when I would visit friends' homes in the OBE state and later in the day tell them who was there and what they were doing at what time. They were rather spooked by me; so I learned to shut up about it.

Well, I finally repaired the old Datsun and once again decided to head back to Michigan, via Georgia, to visit my brother, this was in March 1985. I packed up the Datsun and my dog named Roach, a red Doberman, and hit the road. The truck ran okay, but I barely made it to Atlanta, Georgia. Once in Atlanta, I ended up staying with my pot smoking brother a couple of months. I found an apartment to rent in Norcross and a job down the street at the same chip producers, Atlanta regional warehouse. I was making damn good money for an eighteen year old, high school drop out. Things were going fairly well, until I was approached by the second shift supervisor who asked me for a favor.

He had a brother that lived in Miami and a sister in Macon. Every week or two he would meet his brother at his sister and pick up a couple brief cases full of cocaine. He needed some help getting rid of it, so here I go again. I was the Inventory and Quality Control Specialist for the regional warehouse in Atlanta. Part of my job included taste testing and weighing random samples of snack foods on the digital scales, quality assurance. Every couple of weeks, I'd be weighing out other samples for my boss and making a little better than the average warehouse man. Once again, I allowed myself to step on to that slippery slope of substance abuse.

I worked with a rather culturally diverse crew in Atlanta. There were a few college students, a few good old boys, a few colorful black guys and the token gay man. There was one person in particular who really stood out. His name was Ronnie. Ronnie was twenty-seven, married, with two small kids and going to school to be a Baptist preacher. We worked in a fast paced setting with deadlines to meet. The job could be stressful and often brought out the worst in one's vocabulary. But Ronnie was different, he never cussed. He wouldn't say shit if he had a mouthful. I admired his commitment to God.

One evening, after the cocaine had begun to take its toll on me, I found out my girlfriend was pregnant, the day after I found a picture of her in our bed with another guy. Life was again beginning to suck, so I asked Ronnie a question. "Ronnie, how do you put up with all the grief these guys give you and never cuss? What is your religion all about?" He proceeded to answer as follows: "Phil, if you died right now and stood before God and he asked you why you should get into Heaven, what you would say?" I halfheartedly replied, "Well, I'd say I have done the best I could, given my circumstances and if he didn't understand, oh well." He proceeded as any good Southern Baptist would, John 3:16, "For God so loved the world he gave his only begotten son and he who has faith in him shall never perish, but have life everlasting." He said, "All you have to do is ask Christ into your heart and you will be 'Saved'." So he helped me say a prayer, I didn't really mean, and the next day I was snorting coke. Little did I know he actually did plant a seed. Things grew worse, I lost my job and in a few weeks I was headed back to Michigan, this was in May 1986.

It had been almost three years since I'd seen my parents. While I was gone my parents had moved from our childhood home and built their retirement home here in Stanton, MI. When I walked up the drive and said, "Hi!" to my dad, he didn't even know who I was at first. I ended up staying with them and stayed clean for almost a year. While I was living in the sticks with my folks, we had a chance to get to know each other. I was looking for a job and was having a hard time due to the economy in this rural area. It was very different from Atlanta and San Diego. I needed the change of pace. I managed to find some help getting into school, from a vocational rehabilitation group. This was not a drug rehab thing. They helped me because of the back injuries I sustained while working the warehouse job in Atlanta. I also had bi-lateral scoliosis, spondylosis and a hair line fracture in my L-5 vertebrae. The neurosurgeon suggested lumbar fusion, I declined.

When I went to this voc-rehab place, I had to get a physical and a psych evaluation. After I did, I went to see my counselor and he was astonished when he saw my IQ score. It was, well above average, above requirements for membership in MENSA. Mind you, at this point in time I had a ninth grade education. This guy pulled strings and actually had me enrolled in college before I had my GED. He invited my parents in and pretty much chewed their butts for not recognizing my abilities. So I started college, passed my GED and started to get my life together. But I wasn't ready to waste my time in college, so I quit college to hang out with a few girlfriends and drink a lot of beer.

I enjoyed the time with my dad and the nature. I still had those dreams and the OBE's very regularly. One night something very strange happened. My dad had a fishing buddy, Lou. He worked with my dad for years in the shop and had recently retired; I think he was about fifty-four when he retired. He, my dad and I went fishing quite often on his private lake. We also tipped a few whiskey and waters together. He was an alcoholic, his new marriage was on the rocks and divorce was eminent. The thought of losing his new house on the lake was grinding at him badly, but things seemed manageable, or so we thought.

One night, before one of my niece's weddings, in Detroit, I was asleep and had a very vivid dream. I was out in the ether again, two figures appeared to me. One seemed to be male, the other female. The male figure began to speak to me. "Lou is going to die," he said. I said, "What? But he's only fifty-four and just retired." The male figure stopped me, saying "Phil, this is just how it must be. You need to understand and accept it." I said, "Okay." The next morning I woke up and sat down for breakfast with my parents. I was about to open my mouth and tell my parents about the dream, but I stopped short. The reason being, my mother has always had premonitions about people dying and it always flipped out my dad, so I proceeded to eat my pancakes.

About an hour later, my parents left for the wedding, I left a couple hours after them. When I made it to my sister's, I walked in and saw my mom sitting on the recliner, something was wrong. She looked at me and said, "Lou died." Wow, no way, what a trip. That was freaky. I told my mom about my dream and we both just shook our heads. My mother and I had a shared a freaky experience one morning, a friend of the family died about four years earlier. It was the knock of death. I've had that happen several times. My mom usually smells fresh flowers very strongly, but stranger things do happen.

After the wedding, I returned to mom and dad's and stayed a few more weeks. But living in the sticks was getting to me. I could not find a job and I was not yet ready for college, so I moved back to the Detroit area. You'll never guess what happened after I started hanging out with my old friends. Cocaine again reared its ugly white head. What can I say, it was easy money, but this fight only lasted a few rounds. I moved back to the hood in late February 1987 and by Easter Sunday, I'd had enough. The morning of Easter 1987, I took a friend to Hamtramck to get a large quantity of coke. We returned to the Red Roof Inn, where he was staying, and proceeded to party. That day, I again began to contemplate my existence. In the couple weeks prior, three friends of mine had died: one suicide, one beating death and one shot in the head. I sat there at the inn that day watching all these losers come in and out: people ten to twenty years older than me, wasted lives. I was too good for this.

After staying up all night, coked out, I went into work the next morning, looked my boss in the eyes and said, "I'm a drug addict and I have to get out of this town." I then went to my sister's, where I'd been staying and told her the same thing. I called my sister in South Carolina and asked if I could come down for a week to clear my head. Thankfully she said I could. Then a few minutes later, my brother-in-law called back and said I could stay if I wanted to. Luckily, a week earlier, someone had broken in my car and stole my awesome stereo system from which I had $1500 from the auto insurance to make the trip. I was out of there.

Chapter 4
Going to Carolina

Once again opportunity was knocking and the door wasn't hitting me in the butt. I knew I had to get out of dodge to stop my self-destructive habits. I was intent on changing. There was something significant to that final binge on Easter Sunday. Not only did I realize I was too good to end up like most the losers I was hanging out with that day, but I also remembered what Ronnie had told me about John 3:16. I needed to be "Saved," from myself. So I headed for South Carolina to sincerely ask Christ into my heart.

I arrived in Charleston the first week of May 1987. The second Sunday, May 10th, Mother's day, I went to church. My sister and brother-in-law had not been happy with the church they were attending and were going to try a new one. That Sunday morning we all hopped in the truck and headed out. We arrived at the church about five minutes late. My brother-in-law, being the punctual military man he was, decided he was not going to walk in five minutes after services had started. But, when I looked at the church, I knew I had to go, I'd seen it in a dream. I said, "Look you guys can do what you want, but I'm going in." They reluctantly followed. That morning I went in to the little Southern Baptist church knowing I had to do what Ronnie had told me to do almost a year earlier in that warehouse in Georgia. At the invitation after the service I went up and asked Christ into my heart. The following Sunday, I agreed to be baptized.

That afternoon, I really felt no change in my spirit. But, I knew I was doing the right thing and was determined to follow through. The next Sunday came and I was baptized in water. Know this event, for me, was truly a miracle. I walked into the baptismal a long haired, drug addicted, vengeful person who cared about no one but me, and I obviously didn't care that much. They say that the baptism in water is merely a symbolic gesture. It represents dying to one's old self and coming out anew. For me it was much, much more. I indeed said goodbye to my old self and let it go. I let it all go. When I rose up out of that water I was a new man. The hate and vengeance I had clung to for so many years, was gone. Words truly cannot fully express the changes which occurred in me that day.

Within three months I had finished reading the Bible. I attended every service that church had. I shared my testimony and even gave a sermon in front of the church. I was not only attending Sunday school, I was teaching it. I even joined the choir. Heck! I even got a hair cut. A cuss word barely entered my mind let alone come out of my mouth. Everything I prayed for, I received. It was awesome. But then, I met the young lady I would make my first wife. Love is blind, and often stupid. In January 1988, against the advice of my good friend and preacher, who literally held open the back door of the church on my wedding day and told me to run, I married the mother of my three youngest children.

For eight straight months, I walked very close to God. I was living an exemplary Christian lifestyle, but I couldn't live the exemplary Southern Baptist lifestyle. I truly felt the calling to preach and would have gone to seminary if I had not met my first wife, maybe. However, there were things that religion held to that logic would not allow me to adhere to. Evolution, dinosaurs, dancing, music, I liked my classic rock, and their taking every parable and story from the Bible literally. I mean, a man gets swallowed by a fish and is spit out three days later, come on. There was also the hypocrisy, the upstanding members of the church who drank occasionally, and the deacons who were members of the KKK, and so on. Hell, I even believed in the possibility of life on other planets. I had surpassed the limitations of this religion, but I am thankful for the direction in which it sent me.

After I married my wife, I chose to attend church less often as I had. I held fast to my faith in Christ and stayed clean for years. In December 1988, when my eldest son was a month old, I decided to move back to Michigan to be closer to my parents. So I gave up a decent, but dead end job at General Dynamics; where I worked in the planning department building Trident series nuclear submarines, and moved back to the sticks of Michigan. Yes, I know that was a stupid thing to do, but I had my reasons. There was a slight conflict of interest in my desires to want to help save the human races, while helping build weapons to destroy the planet. And my new wife was never meant to be a mother, nor was her mother. I worked all day and took care of the baby all night. I needed help raising my child and was not going to get it where I was.

Chapter 5
The First Marriage Years

I'm not one say bad things about people, especially the mother of my three youngest children, so I will say this. She was a victim of child sexual abuse and was raised in an alcoholic family. After we married she lost all ambition to do anything with her life. I worked dead end jobs and made enough money to subsist, while she did less and less. The next two children were born in 1990 and 1991. She was supposedly taking birth control pills but they obviously did not work. So we found ourselves with three small children.

After our youngest was born she suffered from postpartum depression. Adding that to her lack of parenting skills, things became even harder for me. I worked 60 or more hours per week and had to come home and clean the house. I tried to get her into counseling and attempted marriage counseling. But the counselors told me there was nothing I could do if she was not willing to help herself. She did not want to help herself. I did the best I could, but when she started being abusive to the kids I had to draw the line. When the baby was five months old, I bought her a bus ticket. She left and had no contact with the kids for over fifteen years, and to this date, she has not seen them.

In 1991, I was twenty-five and a father of four. I had my eldest daughter from my former girlfriend; she lived with her mother. I became a single father of three babies, five months, one and two years old. Although, I had a big family their support was minimal. The only solution my family had was to split up my children between them until I could finish school and then give them back to me. My grandma always said, "If you can't say anything nice about someone, say nothing at all." In September 1991, I was taking 18 credit hours at the community college and raising my kids alone. Did I mention my baby had colic for nine months? It was not easy but I was intent on raising my kids.

The first week of November, I found the courage to ask out a girl from my biology class. She was crazy enough to say yes. However she had her scars, some you could see, and some you could not. She suffered some closed head injuries and never really received the rehabilitation she needed. To make things worse two weeks after we started dating she was in another head on collision and put her head through the windshield of her mom's truck. A secondary closed head injury would eventually make a very tough situation even tougher.

She was only nineteen I was twenty five. She had no children and I had four. Both of us were in school full time. I was living off grants and student loans and she worked part time job. We had very little time alone, my kids were always there. A few nights a month I could get someone to watch the kids and we would go out with her friends. After I had finished at the community college we both transferred to a four year college about fifty miles from our homes and lived another twenty miles north of there. We rented a beautiful home on eighty acres of land in the middle of nowhere. Shortly after we moved, we decided to get married. We attended a supportive church, but we did not have any real close friends in the area.

I still had my occasional dream come true things and out of body experiences, but some other odd things occurred in late 1992 and early 1993. One day, we were at the voc-rehab place, which was helping me with college expenses, and the counselor and I had a strange discussion. Somehow we began discussing religion. At the time, I was still slightly stuck in my Southern Baptist mind set, so I did not give much credence to the input from the counselor. He told me he was a Christian, but he also believed there was more out there which the Bible didn't mention. He told me about a book called the Urantia

Book. This book told the whole story of Christ's life, and how his real name was Joshua Ben Joseph. Blasphemy, I thought; but didn't say that to him. I just blew it off. The student was not yet ready.

A few months later, we found someone to watch the kids and we went on a quick vacation to Georgia to visit my brother. We arrived at my brothers about 6:00 in the evening. After visiting a while we went to bed around 11:00pm. When I tried to go to sleep my head was filled with thoughts I could not stop. I could not shut down, so I found a tablet of paper and started writing. I did not know where this stuff was coming from, but it was good. I started at the beginning of the universe and wrote about how life on this planet was actually planted here by scientists from other planets. How Aliens were here hundreds of thousands of years ago to teach us about culture and life. How they constructed the pyramids but eventually had to leave. They left behind clues, like the pyramids and the statues of

Easter Island. There was much more I could not recall; about twenty pages I had written in the course of four hours or so. Unfortunately, my second wife disposed of it when she left, it was very strange.

When we returned from Georgia the stress of reality began to take its toll on our relationship. If I was not busy with the Social Work Association at the college or doing my volunteer work at the senator's office, I was taking care of the kids. I was very politically active; I even had a political science teacher that wanted me to run for office. He said he had friends in the governor's office that would support me. Thankfully one of my mentors, who had retired from the state government, talked me out of it. The marriage lasted about eight months. It was summer 1993 when she decided she had enough playing mother and always being in my shadow, so she left. I choose to leave out the details of the good, the bad, and the ugly times as there were plenty of all. Had it not been for her I don't know how I would have survived the first couple years of single parenting. We did not sever our relationship on good terms and it was in my best interest to get out of town. I was in my senior year of college in the social work program, but being heart broken and living seventy miles from any family or friends, I wanted to get closer to my support system, even if it wasn't the best.

Once again opportunity was knocking on the door. My brother had come up from Georgia for a summer vacation and said he and his wife would help me out if I wanted to move to Georgia. So I shot down to Athens the following week and spoke with the dean of the school of social work at UGA, and was accepted into their Social Work program. A few weeks later I was on the road again.

Chapter 6
Still Running Away from Me?

The kids and I got to Georgia August of 1993. While we were there it was very hard to adjust to life as a single parent. I'm going give you a real brief summary of the two years I was there. I moved to Athens and attended the University of Georgia. I was very active in the community. I became the vice president and director of education for the local Parents Without Partners; I was a student member of the UGA roundtable. I taught parenting classes for the Athens Child Abuse Counsel and the North Georgia Counsel on Child Abuse. I also helped a doctor friend do music therapy at local hospitals. I started playing guitar and writing music. I even shot over to Nashville, Tennessee and did a couple of cable TV shows. Being a single parent, I had to put that dream on hold but I stayed pretty busy.

In May 1995, the state cut their child care funds for full time students and I could not swing the cost of day care, so I had to quit school. Once again, the people who offered to help recanted. Like I said, "If you can't say anything nice..." I ended up going back to work for a while in Georgia, until a friend of mine made me an offer. She was taking a teaching job in Nashville and wanted to know if the kids and I would like to go with her. Sounded like another knock on the door of opportunity.

We moved to Nashville. I found a low paying job as an assistant warehouse manager and struggled to survive. My friend did help out for a while, but her intentions for us were different than mine. After about seven months on my job, having never missed a day, all three of the kids got sick. I had to take off one day to care for them. The next day I returned to work and had my ass chewed by the general manager because $450,000 in shipments did not get out. I told him if he didn't like the fact I had to care for my kids he could find someone else to replace me, then I walked.

I never said I didn't do foolish things. We ended up moving back to Georgia early 1996. We stayed with my brother a few weeks and then got our own place about fifty miles north of Atlanta. I was working another underpaying job as a warehouse manager. Things were going okay, but thanks to no help from a certain person's spouse, I ended up losing my job. I was very distraught but luckily I still had friends in Georgia.

I had some great friends who were very much naturalists. They lived in the woods; home schooled their kids and grew a lot of their own food. I owe them both a great deal of thanks for where they led me. One day shortly after losing my job, while visiting them we were discussing a book a family member had told them about. They could not remember the name. The book talked about the creation of the universe and the entire life of Jesus. Oh my God, the Urantia book. The one the voc-rehab counselor had told me of four years earlier. It was time I checked this book out.

The next day I went to the local library to inquire about the book. The librarian said she had never heard of it but would look it up anyway. "Wow," she said. "We have five copies, but their all out, although there is one on order and it should be here tomorrow." The next day, I pulled up to the library just as the Fed-Ex guy was leaving. I walked up to the counter to check out the book and was surrounded by four librarians, they had a question. One of them inquired, "We have all worked here a long time and never even knew we had this book. What is it about?" I said, "I really wasn't sure. I guess it was some kind of modern day look at the Bible." Boy was I in for a surprise.

The Urantia book is about 2,000 pages. Well, I was in for quite a read. That evening when I got home I began to read another book that would change my life forever. That evening after I put the kids to bed I sat down in my chair and began to read. I'm not going to discuss all the content of the Urantia book, but I sincerely believe it is worth reading. That evening I finished the forward to the book. It about blew my mind. It was very similar to the things I had written three years ago at my brother's while I was on vacation. From that point on, my life began to get even stranger.

After I finished the forward I tried to go to sleep. I went in my bedroom and lied down. Immediately, I was overcome by a wave of energy. It felt as if I was plugged into a light socket. From head to toe my body began to vibrate intensely. Whoa! I sat up and shook all over. Then I just lied back down and it happened again. "Holy Cow," I thought. "What was going on?" I was slightly scared, yet strangely comfortable. Then I lied back down and fell right to sleep.

The next morning I got up and took the kids to school. I then went home and started to pray. I prayed for guidance and understanding, but it wasn't working. I felt I needed to go somewhere solitary, somewhere away from civilization. But where would that be? Then it came to me, Conyers, Georgia. I heard the stories of this place in Conyers where, in some lady's backyard, a vision of the Mother Mary had appeared. Not that I really cared about that, or even believed it were true. But I thought if this did happen there, maybe this really was Holy ground. That is what I needed, Holy ground. So I made arrangements for a babysitter the next day and decided to give it a shot.

The next morning, August 14, 1996, I dropped the kids off at the sitter's and headed to Conyers. I got off the expressway in Conyers and stopped at the local Waffle House to ask for directions. The waitress told me to head north, about five miles and hang a left, I couldn't miss it. Finally, I could find a solitary place to be alone with God and pray. *Not.* When I pulled up the dirt drive into this lady's backyard I was shocked. There were tour busses and about two hundred or more people walking the grounds. "Oh great! So much for solitude". Oh well, I had driven all the way there so I decided to check it out.

My first stop was at the Holy water well. There I spoke with several ladies who had made the pilgrimage there for the past couple of years. I told them I had come to find a solitary place to pray and was shocked by the number of people there. They laughed, "This is nothing," they said. "Yesterday there was over twenty thousand people here to see the vision of Christ." I just gasped; 20,000 that's a lot of people. There were people there from all over the world, I had no idea. One of the ladies then turned to me and said, "Phil, you could have been born a hundred or even a thousand years ago, but Christ saved his bravest soldiers for these final days."

Suddenly, someone came running up to us and said, "The statue is coming to life." Okay, I thought, I had to see this. I walked down to the lower part of the yard and there stood a life sized concrete statue of the Mother Mary holding the Christ child. It was solid white concrete, not painted.

I stood about ten feet in front and to the left of the statue. People were kneeling down in front of the statue while others gathered around, and then it happened. Two very dark pupils appeared in her eyes and she began to smile. I know the others saw the same thing I did. I went there that day seeking guidance. I wanted to know if the Urantia book was what it said it was; I think I found my answers. I then went up to the house and picked up a paper describing what the vision of Christ revealed to the people that were there the day before. According to the paper, Christ expressed His sorrow over the state of the planet and the pain of all the infants being aborted. These obvious things which would cause any loving being pain; needed to stop. There was one thing He said which still strikes me, "Soon I shall return and you will all return home with gold dust on your hands." I will leave this to your own interpretation.

I returned home that evening with a greater sense of knowing. My doubts about the Urantia book were gone. I will discuss more of the Urantia book at a later point in this book, it's an awesome text. Some other questions were answered that day as well. You see a couple of days earlier I spoke with my brother who lived in Florida, he said they would love for me and the kids to come stay with them. After the events of that day, I decided that whatever I did, it would be okay. So the following week I packed up and moved the kids to Florida before school started.

My brother, his wife and their two kids lived just outside of Tampa. It only took me two days to find a job. I started working third shift for a local pest control company. I had previously been licensed in Michigan to apply restrictive and non-restrictive use of pesticides in both residential and commercial facilities. I ended up killing bugs from Clearwater to Zypher Hills for a few months in Florida. Several strange things happened while I was working at different places. It was my second week on the job when I was heading to my first stop in Clearwater. On the way, the police had the road blocked off and there were people walking all around. It was about 11:00 PM, I took a detour to my first stop at this Chinese restaurant. When I walked in, this Spanish speaking guy started blabbering something about, the Madre. He was talking to me but I had no clue what he was saying. Then this little Chinese guy comes up and says, "He's asking if you have seen the Mother."

Considering the events of the past few weeks I thought this rather strange. Anyway, I'd come to find out why the road block was set up on my way there. A vision of the Mother Mary was appearing on the side of a building just down the street. I went to see it the next day but was not really impressed. A couple of days earlier, a few palm trees had been cut down from in front of this glass faced building. It looked to me as if the trees had kept the sun from fading the glass behind the trees. When they were removed, I guess you could see, what appeared to be the shape of Mary's head. This had nothing on what I'd seen in Conyers.

A few days later, I was at work servicing a bar in Clearwater around 3:30 AM. I had keys and alarm codes to businesses all over the Tampa area. I walked into this fairly large bar with pinball and video arcade games lining the walls, I had this eerie feeling. It was like someone was watching me. About halfway through treating this place something weird happened. Suddenly, all of the pinball and arcade games started sounding off, I about filled my pants. I did what I called, a quick service, on that place. Then I was gone. A week or so later I was at the Pizza Hut in Zypher Hills about 3:00AM, halfway through that job the jukebox kicked on. It started playing Stevie Ray Vaughn, if it were a ghost at least it had good taste in music.

I enjoyed the opportunity to spend time with

my brother and his family and I know they enjoyed my being there. I was basically the only one in the family who didn't ridicule my sister-in-law when she said the aliens took her baby. Like I'd said earlier, I never doubted the existence of ET's. I thought if God could make one planet, why not one thousand more? He had to be able to do better than this. And after reading what I had in the Urantia book the possibility was even more believable. I figured if they were out there and coming to borrow our children, they probably had a good reason. After all our children are not our property, they are our responsibility, they belong to God.

Let me share my sister-in-law's story very briefly. Back in 1993, she was three months pregnant; this was confirmed by the doctor. One night shortly after a doctor visit she claims she was abducted from her bed, taken aboard an alien craft and given a vaginal exam. The next morning she woke up terrified and told my brother what had happened. My brother had been with her for more than ten years and, being open minded, took her word for it. So she went to the doctor and the fetus was gone, I don't doubt her sincerity. About a year after this happened she went to a local TV show where twenty women from the Tampa area claimed the same thing happened to them around the same time.

Oddly enough, while I was there the local news in Tampa ran a week long story on alien abductions. One of the stories was with a lady from the Tampa area who had the same experience as my sister-in-law, but she claimed the aliens would come and pick her up every two to three weeks to help counsel the half human half alien babies on how to deal with their human emotions. Okay. Why not? If these beings are intelligent enough to somehow transverse great distances faster than light, they surely must have evolved enough to have no need to conquer this planet. If they can do what some say, conquering us would be a cake walk. Sure their may be some rogue factions who are self serving, but overall I would think most are peaceful.

After spending some time at my brother's and viewing his small video collection on the whole alien thing, I started to try communicating with them. Basically, I would ask them, if they were listening, to come pick me up and get me off this rock. I guess, at that time, my telepathic communications needed some work.

The kids and I stayed in Florida a couple of months but it just was not working, I had to leave. It was the best thing to do for the kids and myself. Here again, when I can't say too many good things, I choose to say nothing at all. We had conflicting views on child rearing and financial responsibilities. I literally had nowhere to go, but I knew I had to leave. So again I put my faith in God, packed up the kids in the car and split.

My closest destiny was Nashville. I still had true friends there and I believe that's where God wanted me to go. We drove from Tampa to Nashville and showed up on the door step of a good friend. She was a very beautiful woman I had met a few years earlier. Our friends tried to hook us up, but I couldn't. She was too much like a sister to me. Plus, she was a single mom of three young boys and I could not handle them. She put us up a few days, but her boyfriend was very jealous, so we ended up staying in a homeless shelter for about a month.

Why a homeless shelter? Why not just go back to Michigan? At the time I had given up on my family just as they had given up on me, I'll say no more on that subject; therefore, we stayed in a homeless shelter. It was a family shelter and actually wasn't that bad. I had a job the first week back in Nashville; again I landed a warehouse manager position. I had to travel about fifty miles every day. But it was better than sleeping in the car. The kids were in school and I was working. The people at the shelter helped us get into our own place within a month. We survived.

Everything happens for a reason. At least, it does if you make it. Staying in the shelter allowed me to meet some people I probably would not have met. One of those people turned out being very important to me. Not because of a great friendship, but because of a great story. This person was not in the shelter the same time as my kids and I; he was there with his family a few months prior. It just so happens he was living in a low income apartment next door to a friend I met in the shelter. One day while visiting my friend he came over. We were discussing the Urantia book and got on the topic of aliens. That's when he started getting weird.

He started scratching his arms and sweating. His wife looked at him with a strange look on her face. She said, "It's happening, ain't it?" He pulled up his pant leg and said, "Oh yeah!" Then he proceeded with the following. "This happens when ever I start talking about them. What I'm about to tell you.... I got to tell you I don't tell people about this, but since you already believe, here it goes." Now I must interject before I continue with his story. He warned me before he continued. So I will do the same. If you hear this story it may start something you can't stop. It may not be good. Are you ready?

His Story

In 1993 I was in the Marines. I was stationed in Italy where I worked at a top secret base somewhere in the desert. They would blindfold us and take us to work. Look, my wife is right there and she can confirm this, I'll go next door and get my papers to prove I was there. (That was not necessary.) *It was my job to guard this underground facility. The walls were four feet thick concrete. My duty was to stand inside a small room, like a small conference room. I would enter the room turn around and face the thick steel sliding door, a loaded weapon in hand. On the other side, stood another marine who faced the entrance to the facility. Our orders were to kill anything that tried to come through that door without permission. After I worked there a few months, my curiosity started to get to me. One day, I came in and I messed up. There was an old 8mm movie projector, like the ones we had in elementary school, sitting in the room. I knew no one would be there for a while so I flicked it on. I couldn't believe what I saw. It showed another facility similar to ours somewhere in the desert. It started by showing the outside. There were limos and helicopters parked in the field. Then the guy taping, walked down the corridor into the facility. When he got inside it looked like a mini United Nations. There were people from different countries and then the camera turned up to the podium. At the podium there was a little alien. He looked kind of like one of the grays, but he had hair and was a little bit chunkier than the grays. Boy, I flipped out. There was no sound so I couldn't hear what was being said. I shut that thing off and rewound it. I took my post and didn't move. The next night I was home in bed and all of a sudden it felt like someone was sitting on my chest. I was paralyzed, I couldn't move. (This guy was huge. About six* foot five, 240 lbs. He was a big boy.) *I looked up and this little gray dude was doing something to my leg. Then he spoke to me in my head. He said, "This will be a reminder for you to never speak to anyone about what you saw." Then he walked through the wall.*

After he finished with his story he pulled up his pant leg again. It looked like someone just cut his leg open, but it wasn't bleeding. He also had a rash on his arms and chest. He said it happened every time he talked about them. That was quite the story.

So a few days later, after work, I picked up the kids from daycare and pulled up in my drive. It was a very overcast day; the clouds were thick and hanging low. When I was taking the kids in the house I noticed some lights in the sky above my house, it was 4:30 PM. I lived about a mile from the Nashville airport and three miles from the mall. I first thought the lights were somehow coming from one place or the other, but then there were more. These lights were shining down from the clouds. There were four beams blinking intermittently in a circle about forty feet in diameter. There was no sound. Then there were four more lights in a circle, then four more. In all three sets of four lights were right above my house. Then one set disappeared. The other two sets stayed for about an hour. I thought somehow lights from the airport or mall were reflecting off the heavy clouds. But that didn't really make sense, it was a mystery.

The kids and I stayed in Nashville until early May 1997. After a great deal of thought and prayer, I decided to move back to Michigan. It had been six months since I'd contacted anyone in my family. Though I had tried for years to avoid returning to Michigan, I realized it was my destiny. There had always been an underlying cause for my not returning. Earlier, I'd mentioned my dreams that come true, well there was a series of dreams I've had since I was very small; those type of dreams. I cannot tell you how many times they have repeatedly haunted my sleeping hours, the same dreams; dreams of war; the "final" war. It is the war that would take place when I was older. When my children were grown and I was living in Michigan. But over the years, I've learned something about these dreams; I can't hide from them. I would eventually have to face them as they were my destiny, or so I thought.

Chapter 7
Going Home Again

Once again, I rented a U-Haul and headed north. We arrived in Michigan and stayed at one of my sister's. It was not the most desirable place to be, but it was better than the homeless shelter, almost. My sister loved us and took us in. I enrolled the kids in school to finish out the year, and found a part time job. My car had died before I left Nashville so finding a decent job was not easy. In June, I found a construction job I was to start in July; then I broke my ankle. While I was recovering from my injury, I had spent as much time as I could at a friend's house near Flat Rock. She was great to me and the kids and it gave us a safe haven away from my sister's.

One night my nephew and I went to visit her while my sister watched the kids. That evening we had been discussing the alien topic. As my nephew and I were leaving her house, around 11:00 PM we noticed something in the sky, actually it was several things. Way up in the sky, about as high as the commercial jets flew as they were coming in to Detroit Metro, there were nine things bopping around. They maneuvered unlike anything I'd ever seen. "Check that out, Uncle Phil," my nephew screamed, as he pointed to the sky, I already was. They darted back and forth in every direction for about three minutes. Then I saw one of them take off, in a split second it vanished, leaving behind it a streak of green light. Suddenly the rest of them just disappeared. I looked at my nephew and said, "Adam I think we just seen some UFO's."

A week later we were visiting my friend again and left her house about 10:00 PM. On the way home, we were both intently watching the sky. I was driving home on the back roads. As we started turning into a large curve, I noticed a bright light through the trees near the river. What's that? The next thing I recall we were about two miles further down the road at a stop sign. I looked over and my nephew was sleeping. I yelled at him to wake up. Then I asked him how we got there. We simultaneously said, "We were just abducted." I don't really know that we were, nor does he. It was a very strange feeling.

A few days later, I was jamming at another friend's house a couple of blocks away from my sister's. I left his place at 10:00 PM and started hobbling home. About 10:10 PM, I was in the school yard just behind my sister's house. It was a very stressful time and I couldn't wait for my ankle to heal so I could get back to work. I was in the middle of the field behind the school when I suddenly had a strange sensation. I felt so dang happy, I felt elated and loved. Something was not right. I looked up and about 30 feet above my head a craft was hovering silently, it was awesome. It was a glowing a silver metallic color and was egg shaped with deep grooves on its underside. Then without a sound it took off. When it did it left a tube of bright white light, about 8 feet in diameter, behind it. The tube of light was similar to the contrail of a jet, but it first appeared almost solid then turned into a cloud, finally vanishing. As the craft took off, it flew approximately fifty yards to the edge of the field at an altitude of about 30 feet. It then took a sharp turn about 80 degrees straight up and disappeared into the night sky. The exhaust trail followed it all the way.

"Okay God," I said, shaking my head in utter amazement. "What is up with that?" I stayed out in the field for a while watching the sky. I went into my sister's at about 10:45 PM. I felt no fear; on the contrary, I felt nothing but peace. It was a beautiful sight. Little did I know it was far from the last sighting I would have.

By August my ankle was healed and I found a job as an assistant home supervisor at a crisis center for developmentally disabled adults. By September, I saved enough money to move into my own place in Howell. I worked midnights at the home and in the spring of 1998 I started a part time job doing pest control in the mornings. Eventually I quit the midnight job at the home and started to do pest control full time. It's kind of ironic that I could make more money killing bugs than I could by caring for humans.

There were several strange things that happened while I was living in Howell. First let me start to tell you about the fish. After we moved in to our house I bought the kids a fish tank and three baby cichlids. The kids loved the fish. So I went back to the fish store and bought a scum sucker to help clean the tank. A couple of days later the scum sucker and two of the cichlids were dead and Goldie, the pseudotroepheus zebra was looking pretty ill. The kids were heartbroken so I actually prayed for Goldie to survive and she did. She did; however develop a strange purple mark near her belly, and more, which I will discuss later.

The U.F.O. sightings began to intensify. I have seen a lot of different types of flying craft which are capable of maneuvering and traveling unlike anything the human race has yet developed; as far as I am aware. Fifteen years or so, after I had the close encounter behind my sister's house in the schoolyard; I've had dozens, if not, hundreds of day time sightings. Often times I can call them out, if I ask nicely. I do have witnesses who will testify to this. I will discuss the subject in detail later. But I'm not going to give details on every sighting I've had; that would take another entire book. When I was doing the pest control in Howell and the surrounding areas in 1998, I saw them very often.

There were times I'd see them in the same area around the same time three or more days in a row, especially around the time the kids' fish died, I'll explain the possible connection later. Work was going well and I made a lot of money for my boss. Every weekend, I was not working I would head up to my folks' house to help them out. In the late summer of 1998, I decided to move closer to my folks. My boss said he would help me start my own pest control business near my folks' house if I wanted, therefore, I did. In September, we found a house and moved up state.

I made plans to start up the business in the spring of 1999 when the bugs started coming out. Spring came and the business took off. I had finally started to make a decent living. Things were finally starting to smooth out. When summer came my boss began to get very busy in Howell and he needed some help. So I decided to stay down there a few days a week, and do my work at home on the other days and weekends. And that is what I did from late June until the first part of August 1999. The kids and I stayed at my friend's near Howell, I worked and she baby sat. It worked out fairly well.

It was August 6, 1999; I woke up ready to head back home. My work in Howell was done. I helped my boss get caught up and I had customers waiting back home. It was a beautiful day. Then the phone rang. It was my boss. He needed me to do him one small favor before I left. He wanted me to do three quick jobs before I left. I agreed. So I got my gear around and headed out about 10:30 A.M. I stopped at the gas station then at McDonalds; then I headed to my first job.

I was about five miles from McDonalds, the sun was shining, I had both hands on the wheel and was driving 55 mph: the speed limit. Someone was riding my tail, but I was in no hurry. I was heading north and a big gravel truck went flying by heading south. To the west I saw this guy jogging out of his friend's yard waving goodbye to her. There was another car heading south, toward me, in the opposite lane. Well, I guess this jogger thought he could beat the car heading south, so he darted out into the road. He did beat that car, but he crossed the yellow line about 5 feet in front of my truck.

I hope that August 6, 1999 will always be the worse day of my life. I always think of the Simpsons' episode where Marge ran over Flanders, whenever I think about that day. Right after Marge ran over Ned she said, "God, please let it be a dog." That is exactly what I thought; even though the guy, who killed himself on the front of my truck, looked directly at me after he crossed the yellow line. I still can see this big yellow lab crossing that road. This is definitely one of those stories where I leave out the details. There were four witnesses, including his friend; all of them said he never looked. There was nothing I could do. It doesn't change what is or what it was. Accidents happen. Should of, could of, would of, don't equal did.

Just when I thought things were going to go smoothly, not a chance. They say God never gives you more than you can handle, but this was almost not the case. It was not easy. It was hell. I came very close to losing it. Were it not for my parents, I would have lost the house. Were it not for my friends, I would have lost my mind. I could not sleep, eat or think. I knew better than to ask why. This is a Bible verse I've often turned to in hard times, it's one of the few I'll always remember, Romans11:33, "Oh the depths and the riches of the wisdom and the knowledge of God. How unsearchable His judgments, His paths beyond tracing out. Who has ever known the mind of the Lord? Who has ever been His counselor? Who has ever given to God, that God should repay him? For from Him to Him and through Him are all things. To Him be the glory, forever and ever. Amen."

Chapter 8
Fish and Aliens
Along the Road to Recovery

The events of Fall 1999 impacted my life in numerous ways; in fact it impacted the lives of many people in numerous ways. But it is not the intention of this book to delve into the complexities of the ripple effects of that day. I could make the generalized statement, "You can imagine how it would affect your life", but that statement would be false. You can, perhaps, imagine the horror or even sympathize with me. If you have had a similar experience you may even be able to empathize with me. But you will never understand how I perceived the event. And that is okay. It really messed me up for a while. And that is okay, because everything happens for a reason.

After the accident I went against my better judgment, and became involved with my friend who babysat for my kids that summer. We had a utilitarian relationship. She was willing to help me through the hard times and I needed help. I was numb. I was emotionally distraught and spiritually drained. I went to counseling and tried every type of anti-depressant on the market, nothing eased the pain. Sleep was the closest I came to comfort, but even that was haunted by vivid recollections of the accident. But, I have survived. So let me return to the strange and common events I have grown accustomed to in my daily life.

A week after the accident we all went back to my home up north; my three children and I, my friend and her two children. While I was down state, another friend of mine had been staying at my house keeping up the yard and feeding the fish. A few minutes after I came home I checked on Goldie, the Cichlid I purchased for the kids when we lived in Howell. The fish I prayed for. There were three small fish in her tank. I first thought they were gold fish, which I often fed to Goldie. After a closer look I noticed they were not. I called my friend and asked if he had purchased some other Cichlids and put in the tank. He denied it. He had no idea where they came from. I was greatly puzzled.

Let me tell you a little about Goldie. I had raised different types of Cichlids since I was a kid and had never had them reproduce. Goldie appeared to be a pseudotreapheus zebra, male. Goldie was extremely aggressive. No other fish regardless of size survived in her tank with her more than an hour. When I purchased her she was about two months old as well as the Jack Dempsey and the Firemouth I purchased at the same time, all of them too young to reproduce. Remember, shortly after I bought Goldie the other fish died. After I moved to Stanton I purchased two smaller Cichlids and tried to keep them in the tank with Goldie. She killed them both within an hour. After their death I put nothing in the tank with Goldie accept feeder goldfish. When I returned home in August 1999, Goldie had been the only Cichlid in her 40 gallon tank for more than eight months. I had no other fish in the house accept feeder goldfish and feeder guppies, which I kept in separate tanks. So where did these three small fish come from?

The first thing I did was to call the local pet store. The owner thought I was nuts. She said someone had to have put them in the tank as a joke. Knowing this was no joke I proceeded to investigate. It took some work, but I finally contacted a professor of Ichthyology who was retired from Michigan State University. After I told him what had happened, and after he quit laughing, he grilled me. He kept asking, "Who put you up to this?"   When I finally assured him it was no joke he told me of his work with Cichlids. He had spent four years at Lake Malawi in Africa raising and studying Cichlids. Never, had he heard of a parthenogenetic Cichlid. He then put me in Touch with his former student whom was an ichthyologist at Boston University.   I sent DNA samples of Goldie and the Babies to Boston University, but still have never heard anything on the results.

Goldie died in the spring of 2003. Before she died she had four separate clutches totaling twenty-three offspring. At one point I had twelve fish tanks set up all over my house, trying to separate the babies and keep them alive. Channel 13 news from Grand Rapids and Channel 3 news from Kalamazoo both did stories on Goldie. UPN 50 out of Detroit even ran the story. The first time the story aired was the same day Vice President Dick Cheney had his heart surgery. It was rather funny seeing the Vice President's story, being followed by the story of my parthenogenetic pet fish. It is sad that despite my efforts to give the babies to zoos and aquariums around the country, they ended up killing each other off and dying of other fish related diseases in my home.

To the best of my Knowledge I am the only person to ever have possessed a Cichlid which was capable of cloning its self. At least I am the only person to ever document this unusual event. I need to add a few notes here to spur your curiosity. The strange purple mark that Goldie developed on her belly, shortly after surviving the event in Howell, eventually grew to the end of her tail and then disappeared. However, it was not completely gone until after her final clutch of offspring hatched. There are also the continued UFO sightings I had throughout Goldie's life. Every time, within a few days of Goldie spawning more offspring, I had unusually clear and close sightings of UFOs.

On October 17th, 1999 I had a very spectacular sighting of three huge cigar shaped ships only four miles away from my home. This was one week after I found twelve more babies in Goldie's tank. This is a neat little story I need to share. It was 1:15 PM; my friend was driving us to the store. She and I had been together for several sightings of UFOs so another sighting would not have been a real surprise. The sky was clear as we headed west out of town. As we were going through a series of curves in the road I noticed something in the sky through the tree line. I thought it was just a commercial jet, but, jokingly said, "Look it's a UFO". As we came through the final curve past the tree line the road straightened out for a good mile and a half with open fields on both sides. We looked to the south, at an altitude of about 100 feet there were two huge cigar shaped ships only 50 feet from the roadside. One of the ships immediately hopped to the north side of the road. The other ship sped off straight to the west and was out of sight in 30 seconds.

The ship that was now to the north of us remained at an altitude of around 100 feet and kept pace with us as we slowed and headed west. We went about a half mile and I had her stop at the party store so I could run in and grab a soda. As I left the car and headed toward the store a lady was coming out. I stopped and said, "Have you ever seen a UFO?" I then pointed to the huge craft hovering over the store. She gasped, "Oh My God", she said, "What is that?" Shrugging my shoulders and smiling, I said, "I don't know, I see them all the time." Then I just walked in and grabbed my soda. When I came out, that poor lady was still staring at the hovering craft as it slowly headed west. I hopped back in the car and we proceeded west. Suddenly, another similar craft appeared out of the north and high tailed it out of there as if to catch up with the other two ships. I still wonder what affect the sighting had on that lady.

The girl that was living with me was somewhat obsessed with the alien thing and was always thinking she was getting abducted, as if it were some grand privilege. Whenever she had a little unexplained bruise or mark on her body she would try to relate it to the aliens.

The evening I stood at the sink doing the dinner dishes and I thought out to the Aliens, "Hey, if you guys are out there and you can hear me, do me a favor. Since the accident I have been a wreck. I've tried taking all this dope from the doctors, the anti-depressants and anti-anxiety pills. They don't help. If there is something you can do, would you mind?" I tried to go to bed at 11:30 P.M. that night. I say tried here because sleep did not come easy for me after the accident. I usually sat up for hours watching T.V. and crying. The stupidest things would set me off. So that night I lied down in my bed, the alarm clock said 11:33. I closed my eyes. I turned over and looked at the alarm clock. It was 12:47. Wow! I couldn't believe it. I actually slept an hour and don't even remember trying to fall asleep.

The next morning I woke up and slipped on my long john shirt and went to my folks to cut some wood. That evening I came home and started to get into the shower. As I pulled off my shirt, I caught a glimpse of a very dark bruise on the back side of my right arm, just below my tricep. Being the smart ass I am, I ran out to the girl that lived with me and said;

"NOW THAT'S AN ABDUCTION BRUISE." As I twisted my arm to show her and take a closer look, a small pellet like object surfaced in the center of the bruise. I started flipping out. The bruise was a very dark donut shaped circle. It was about an inch and a quarter in diameter; with a quarter inch circle in the middle that was not bruised. In the center of the un-bruised circle is where the pellet was.

That's when I really began to question what these aliens were up to. I grabbed a razor blade knife and seriously contemplated removing the object. It was sub-dermal, not intra-muscular, but there was a lot of skin to slice through. So the next day I started my quest for answers. At the time I did not have internet access so I began at the local library. Eventually I found some information on MUFON. I was fortunate enough to have some very kind and understanding investigators come out to the house the following weekend. Neither of them were experiencers nor had they ever had a UFO sighting themselves. But they helped me get in touch with a wonderful group of people who were experiencers. This was a small group of people who met at one of the member's homes. Though most of them were familiar with MUFON, not all were members. A few weeks later I attended a meeting that would forever enhance my life.

I've intentionally not mentioned names of friends and acquaintances throughout this book to maintain their anonymity. Here I make an exception. When I met this wonderful group of average Americans, I realized I was not alone. I still consider all of them friends and on a grander scale, family. Though we may go years without speaking, they will always be my family.

There is one person in particular who I must mention, Marilyn. When Marilyn met me she said she could see an intense aura which surrounded me. She could feel the energy I gave off. She told me of a friend of hers, she thought I would be interested in meeting, Dr. Levengood. Were it not for Marilyn I may never had met the greatest mentor I've ever had. My Giant, Lefty. Although I waited almost a year to meet him because, "the student was not ready."

At the meeting that day, I met a group of successful, ordinary people whom all shared an extraordinary secret. They all had stories of alien encounters, some of them were able to recall their events through hypnosis; others just woke up on alien craft in the middle of experimental medical procedures, no hypnosis necessary.

Until recently, I have had no conscious recollection of physical contact with alien beings. And I am not comfortable with the hypnosis thing for myself. I'm too stubborn to let any one into my mind. So, until I have actual conscious contact with an alien being, I will not state that I am a contactee. Yes, I have seen their ships, not the ships pilots. I do not discount hypnotherapy; nor, the success people have dealing with their experiences through hypnosis. It has been a helpful tool for many, but I'm still a bit too clinically challenged to apply it to my own experiences.

After my first meeting, I attended several MUFON functions and learned more about the whole alien thing. I met more wonderful people who have become wonderful friends. They helped me through some very trying times. A couple of months after my first meeting I had another implant experience. The sightings were occurring fairly regularly throughout the year 2000. One morning I woke up and came downstairs with my shirt off and my friend noticed a strange slice on my back near my spine. She rubbed it and both of us could feel something. It felt like a pencil lead approximately one half inch long had been placed under the skin on my back just to the right of my T-11 vertebra. I called an ET contactee friend and asked her how I could know if THEY were responsible. She said, "Just ask them."

That evening before I went to bed I derived a

question. I had my friend take an ink pen and mark my back above and below the object in my back. Then I asked THEM, "If you are responsible for this object in my back, sometime during the night, I want you to make a mark on my back between the two lines". The next morning I woke up, and guess what; a big red line right where I asked for it; right between the lines. It was weird.

I still don't know why the implants are there or what they're for; but they're still there. I did see my doctor about the thing in my arm a couple of days after it happened. When I told him what happened, he replied, "I hope they're not picking you up. They pick up the guy I buy my blueberries from and he says they can be pretty nasty. My mother has been a member of MUFON for years." He could feel and see the object under my skin. He ordered an X-ray, but nothing showed up on it.

In the Spring of 2005 one of my daughters injured her wrist on the playground. She was fifteen years old at the time. When the doctors X-rayed her wrist, they could see a small metal pellet lodged deep in her wrist, near the bone. The head of the X-ray department and the emergency room doctor could not explain it; and did not want to discuss it. I raised my daughter her entire life and I know she never injured herself in a manner that would explain a metal object embedded in her arm.

I have much more to discuss on the topic of ET's or I.D.'s, "inter dimensional beings." They have been a continuous presence in my life for years and I will explain how shortly. For now, however, I want to turn the focus of this discussion toward energy, bio-intrinsic energy to be more specific.

Please see the Afterword section of this book to view U.F.O. sketches and fabduction mark photos.

Chapter 9
Meeting My Giant

Ever since Marilyn told me about Dr. Levengood in 1999, I wanted to meet with him. It just took some time for me to make an effort. I heard of his work from several other friends and I heard of his supposed attitude. I was told he could be a bit moody, not to talk about religion or God, and if he likes you, he likes you, if he don't, he don't. Well you can't always believe what you hear. I finally gave him a call in November of 2000 and made arrangements to go to his house.

Before I went to Dr. Levengood's home I knew little about his work. I knew he did research on crop circles, cattle mutilations and dust samples from the homes of supposed abductees. Most people have heard of the crop circles and cattle mutilations, but not too many know of the dust samples. Lefty called them pseudo crystals. They were originally found when an E.T. experiencer noticed a layer of dust on her recently cleaned floor, shortly after a UFO beamed the room with light. She collected samples on a cotton swab and sent them to Lefty. Further research showed similar pseudo crystals in dust samples collected from the homes of several E.T. experiencers. Here are a few samples taken from my home in December, 2000.

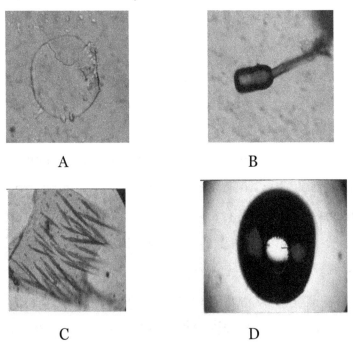

A

B

C

D

These samples were collected on the tip of a cotton swab; none of these objects were visible with the naked eye. The first three objects, A, B and C are magnified 450 times. The fourth, object D was magnified 40 times. According to Lefty, object A is the shell of a sphere made from some sort of pseudo crystal material. Object B, is a common pseudo crystal. Objects C and D are just strange.

The pseudo crystals were interesting, but that was not what interested me most. It was his work with the device which measured the bodies' bio-intrinsic energy field. The reason I was so interested in the CDP device was my Grandfather. When I was about twenty I learned my Grandfather, my father's father, was a faith healer. He offered to teach my mother how he did his healing, but she was afraid. The family secret was lost, until, after years of prayer and luck, I found it again. I learned how Grandpa did a few things, but the scientist within me needed proof. I had done things, healing things, but wrote it off to potential coincidence. I hoped this Dr. Levengood could shed some light on the subject. I would soon find out.

I arrived at Dr. Levengood's lab, and we hit it off. One of the first things we discussed is not calling him Dr. Levengood; so from here on, I will try to refer to him as Lefty, which was his preference. We talked for some time to get acquainted; then we got down to business. Lefty explained how Dr. Gedye and he developed the CDP device. He explained how the Charge Density Pulse device was capable of measuring bio-intrinsic energies in plants, animals and humans. He told of others who he had experimented with using the device and how persons who were hands on healers and some ET experiencers tended to have higher energy readings than others. He told me of a certain individual, Edd, who was an ET experiencer and a healer who had actually set off the device from over 500 miles away. Edd is quite attuned to his energy and capable of controlling it fairly well. On average most people register between 1 and 2 milliamps. Edd was measuring well above these levels. After working with the CDP a while Edd could actually turn his energy levels up and down at will. Now it was my turn.

The CDP prototype, at that time consisted of two aluminum plates, with wires running through the CDP junction box into a chart recorder. Lefty asked me to stand in front of the plates and, when he said okay, to place my hands gently on the plates. I stood up in front of the plates and thought, or prayed, "Okay Lord, Let's show this old fart what we got". Lefty, turned the chart recorder on and said, "Okay."

I placed my hands on the plates. The chart recorder screeched. "JESUS CHRIST", Lefty said. I pulled my hands off thinking I broke his machine. Lefty said, "NO, NO, You didn't have to take your hands off of it, I just never had to turn down the sensitivity before." I went off scale, well over 10 milliamps. We waited a few minutes and tried again with the device set a less sensitive setting. I tried again and came darn close to 20 milliamps. Lefty was quite astonished. We waited a while and talked some more about Edd and how Edd was eventually able to control the energy flow. So I decided to give it a shot. Lefty said, "Now don't get too cocky. It took Edd a while to get used to turning it up and down. I don't want you to get discouraged". I said, "Hey, if I can do it I will; if not, no big deal." We began another trace and on Lefty's cue I turned it up, it worked. Then he said shut it off, and I did. Holy Cow, this thing worked. I was amazed. My grandpa could do the things I heard of. Heck I could do the things I thought I could do. Finally I had proof. I had scientific proof.

If you want to see the patent on the CDP device, STOP NOW, and go on line to: www.uspto.gov, then go to patents, then to patent search by number and type in patent # 6,347,238. This will pull up the patent for the CDP device. I will describe our work with the CDP device and its practical applications in greater detail later. For now, let's get back to the story.

The first day I spent at Lefty's was one of the most fulfilling days of my life. It was a day of confirmation. That day strengthened my beliefs in so many things, most importantly, faith in myself. The world now had a new means of measuring bio-intrinsic or subtle energies.

That night when I returned home, my brain hurt. It took several days for all the information to sink in. Heck, some information is still sinking in and it has been years since that day. Even though it hurt my brain, I couldn't wait to go back. So a couple of weeks later I returned to the lab. My second day at the lab we did more cool stuff. We started by taking my CDP traces. Then Lefty had me hold a large piece of glass in front of my face and he took pictures. He was testing something he calls the red eye effect; it has to do with high CDP energy levels and red eyes in photographs.

Lefty then had me try and put out the flame on a candle. I didn't quite put it out, but I came close. I felt like I was starting my Monks' training. He also had me hold some large crystals to see if I could pick up anything from them. He wanted to see if I could tell him something about their history. Then Lefty took out the Roswell Metal; which is actually part of the legendary Art Bells, Art's parts. A friend of Lefty's, Linda, received it from a person who had stated that they were on clean up detail for the Army at the sight of the Roswell Crash in 1947. That is the story I heard from Lefty. The metal has very unique characteristics. It is derived of several compounds which are microscopically layered. I held the metal in my hands for ten minutes and it increased my bio-intrinsic energy levels significantly.

Subsequent CDP trace studies conducted with the Roswell Metal showed similar results with numerous individuals. When the metal is held in one

116

manner it tends to increase the bio-intrinsic energy field; when held in another manner the metal decreases or completely stops the flow of bio-intrinsic energies. Several years ago Lefty discovered that the metal was also a bio-degradable source of hydrogen gas. Lefty had some cool things in the lab from time to time.

When I returned home after my second visit to the lab, things started getting even stranger than normal. All of the information had begun to sink in on a much deeper level. I finally began to realize, and accept, who I was and what I was capable of. For a couple of weeks my newly discovered energy was very erratic. The TV and lights would turn on and off by themselves, doors would slam shut, glasses would shatter; it was strange. I began to truly realize the power of thought. Now all I had to do was learn how to harness the energies. This is a skill which must surely be mastered.

Since my first two journeys to the lab, there

have been many more, each visit producing remarkable events. I would like to touch on a couple of those things here. Earlier I had mentioned the red eye effect, Lefty believes there is a correlation between this and **light amplification** through **stimulated emissions** of **radiation**, LASER. So he devised an experiment with a laser beam and the CDP device to see if it were possible to affect a laser beam with a person's CDP energies. My eldest daughter was the first to try the experiment. Lefty set up a laser beam so that it reflected off a mirror, ran between two small aluminum plates, which carried the CDP energies of my daughter, then shone on a graph about 8 feet away. My daughter stepped up to the CDP device and waited for Lefty's signal. He started the chart recorder and asked her to place her hands on the plates. Screech! Lefty looked at me shaking his head and quietly mouthed out, *"Jesus* Christ." Shaking his head and smiling he said aloud, "She is your daughter." She had a rather high CDP energy level but more importantly she moved the laser beam. I was the next to try the experiment and the same results occurred, when the CDP energies passed from one aluminum plate to the other the laser beam moved with the direction of energy flow.

About a year later I took my new girlfriend, Holly with me. I had to assure her Lefty was a real person not just an imaginary friend. Lefty put Holly through the usual experiments. While we were there Lefty had something new he had wanted me to see. Our colleague Edd had sent Lefty some rocks. The rocks were from Georgia, they had a small amount of poor quality quartz crystal in them. What was unique about them was that Edd had energized these rocks with his CDP or implicate energies and they turned purple. Lefty explained why they turned purple; it was something about the crystalline structure of the rocks. Anyway; Lefty asked both Holly and I to hold the rocks in our hands and see if we felt anything from them. Before I proceed I need to give you a little background on what I knew at this point.

Lefty had a friend Joyce Haggelthorn; she was a very lovely lady whom I had the pleasure of meeting one day. Joyce had a very unique CDP trace, while most peoples CDP trace gives off a very sharp point at its peak amplitude; Joyce's trace would plateau or flatten at its peak amplitude. One day while Joyce was working with Lefty, he took Joyce's wedding ring off her finger and placed it on the stem of a geranium. Lefty had taken numerous CDP traces from geraniums and new what to expect as a baseline. Joyce had worn that wedding ring over 50 years, it had a long time to absorb Joyce's implicate energies. When Lefty took the CDP traces from the geranium that had Joyce's ring on its stem the traces began change, showing plateaus similar to those of Joyce's CDP trace. Keep this in mind.

Lefty told me about Edd the first day we met. Edd is the guy with a lot of energies and he has good control of them. I had asked Lefty for Edd's phone number numerous times, but Lefty refused to give it to me. Lefty was just watching out for me. He did not want Edd getting cocky with me or trying to light my butt on fire. Lefty felt Edd was very competitive and not comfortable with people who shared his abilities, or at least came close. I just wanted to talk with Edd and ask how he learned to control his energies and basically just shoot the bull. Lefty did his best to deter our meeting, but that day Lefty screwed up.

Keeping in mind what I've just told you about Joyce's wedding ring holding her trace energies; now let's return to the story. Lefty gave Holly and me the rocks Edd had energized to see what we felt. Immediately it clicked in my head, "I have Edd's energy in my hand." Instantly, the hair on my arm stood straight up. I looked at Lefty and nodded my head. Then I thought the following, "Hi Edd! You don't know me, but I'm a friend of Lefty's and I was wondering, if you weren't too busy, could you please go to the phone right now and call Lefty?" I repeated this three times in my head. The phone rang. I looked at Lefty and said, "That's Edd." Lefty answered the phone, on speaker. "Lefty, it's Edd. Just got in the door coming from Walmart and something told me I had to give you a call." Who needs cell phones? That is how I first managed to speak with Edd. Sure you can call it coincidence, or chance or maybe not.

A couple of weeks later I called Edd, using a telephone, and asked him how he sent the energy to people. He basically told me that, "he created a ball of energy in his head and bounced it side to side, until the energy builds up and then he sends it out." That is all I got. This happened in 2003, a great deal has happened since then; the CDP research his produced some very interesting data and Edd has done some really neat research with the Rhine Research Center in Virginia. Let me tell you about one of the experiments Edd was involved with, before I discuss further CDP research.

I spoke with Edd on the phone one day back in

2003-2004 and he told me about an experiment he was involved in with some type of human photon emission bio-field detection apparatus, at the Rhine Research Center. I do not have the specific details on exactly how the experiment is conducted, but I will do my best to explain my understanding of it.

I believe the subject sits in a dark room and, 'does their thing,' meditation, prayer, Qi gong, Reiki, or 'Edd like things,' and they try to emit bio-intrinsic energies, qi or universal life energies from their bodies. I believe, the device measures photons which can be emitted from the energy workers third eye chakra, the heart chakra, or the la gong qi channels, located in the center of the palms of the hands. There has been a great deal of research in this field which is proving to be very interesting. According to Edd, when they conducted the tests on him, he increased the photon emission to a very high level for a longer time, than any other energy workers tested to that point in time including, Qi gong practitioners, Reiki masters and Buddhist monks. These are very low photon emissions, not visible to the human eye, but measurable with the proper scientific instrumentation. Photons are light energy that can be particles or waves. Yes there is scientific data suggesting that some humans have the ability to emit low levels of photon energy from or through their bodies. If we are emitting photons, are we also emitting quarks and Leptons? Or are we emitting the energy field which determines what quarks and leptons will become? If so, then what is this energy field? Is it possibly related to the Higgs Boson? I think there is a direct relationship. Later, I will explain what I believe the connection is.

The CDP device measures what Lefty referred to as charge density pulse energies or plasmas. I believe David Bohm referred to them as implicate energies; I will refer to these energies as bio-intrinsic or subtle energies; meaning these are the energies that exists in all living things. However, I believe these energies also exist in all things; not just the things we consider to be living. We may not be certain what these subtle energies are, but some people can connect with, and channel these subtle energies; sending them through their bodies to other people. Some people can even send the energies across space/time instantly; be it two feet, two hundred miles, or two thousand miles.

Supposedly nothing travels faster than the speed of light, well what about the speed of human thought, or volition. When the energy healer sends the energy across space/time it arrives to the recipient instantaneously, this has been proven repeatedly with data collected using the CDP device. The following are a few CDP traces I have accumulated over the past 13 years conducting research on numerous human subjects, with the CDP device.

Research with several energy healers, including several Reiki Masters, has produced evidence indicating certain individuals have the ability to intentionally increase and decrease the amount of bio-intrinsic energies emitted through their selves. These CDP traces showed a correlation between the intent of the subject to change the amount of energies flowing through them and both increases and decreases in energy levels, respectively, which were measured, in milli-amps, with the CDP device. Several persons were able to increase their energies and bring their CDP traces to distinct levels and maintain those levels for extended periods of time. Traces were also taken on persons while receiving energy treatments. These traces showed distinct changes in the subject's energy levels as the energy healer progressed with the therapy. After treatment the subject felt better and had scientific data showing an increase in their overall bio-intrinsic energies.

Volition and CDP Traces

The following two graphs show CDP traces taken on a 55 year old female.

Graph # 1 Baseline CDP measurement.

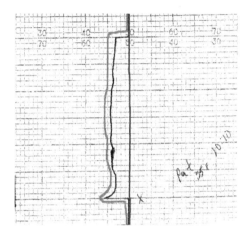

Graph # 2 Subject uses volition to increase bio-field energies when asked to do so by investigator Point (A).

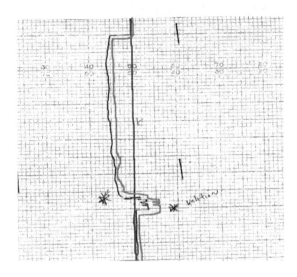

The following pages contain CDP traces of an individual receiving a Reiki treatment from a Reiki master. Note the various changes in the subject's bio-field energies as the Reiki master progresses with the treatment.

This is the CDP trace taken prior to the Reiki treatment. This subject's CDP trace is unusually high. Most CDP traces can be taken with the CDP device set at 10 milliamps. With this subject the CDP device had to be set at 20 milliamps. This is due to the fact that this subject's initial Peak Amplitude (PA) was 15 milliamps, which is off scale on the 10 milliamp setting. At 30 seconds into the CDP trace their PA value was at 8 milliamps and climbing toward the (-) polarity.

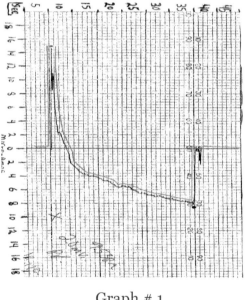

Graph # 1

This section of the CDP trace was taken at the

beginning of the Reiki treatment; Point (A) showing the rapid adjustment of bio-field energies as the Reiki master passes her hands 2 feet above the subject's body to smooth the bio-field energies.

50 seconds into the treatment, (B) the level of the subject's CDP trace has decreased to 3 milliamps and the overall activity has smoothed.

A   B

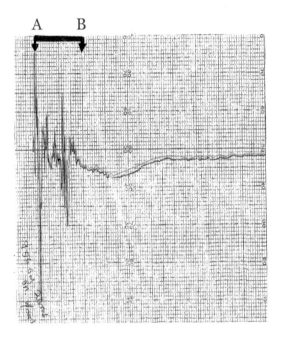

Graph # 2

This section of the CDP trace was taken at 2 through 3 minutes into the Reiki treatment. Point (A) indicates the time the chart recorder was set at 10 milliamps. Point (B) indicates time the chart recorder was switched to the 5 milliamp setting. By increasing the sensitivity of the chart recorder we can better observe the fine structure of the CDP trace. Note that after 3 minutes of Reiki the value of the subject's CDP trace has decreased to 1 milliamp.

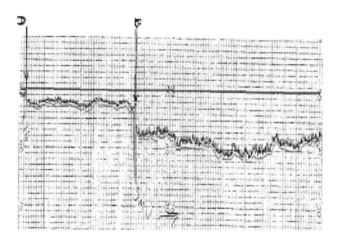

Graph # 3

This section of the CDP trace was taken at 25 through 26 minutes into the Reiki treatment. The subject's baseline CDP trace remained near 1 micro amp for about 22 minutes at this point. Take special note of points A and B. Both of these spikes occurred as the Reiki master made the Reiki Masters Symbol over the head of the subject.

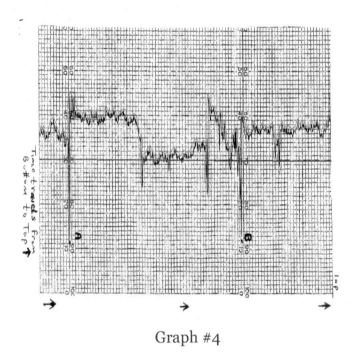

Graph #4

Through careful observation of this subject's entire CDP trace one can conclude that before the Reiki treatment the subject's baseline CDP trace was about 8 milliamps. After less than two minutes into the Reiki treatment the subject's baseline had reduced to about 1 milliamp. This reduction in energy levels resulted in an overall greater feeling of relaxation for the subject.

Perhaps the most interesting observation can be noted in Graph #4, where the 2 milliamp energy spikes occur simultaneously as the Reiki master makes the masters symbol above the subject's head at points (A) and (B).

Notice that when the Reiki master makes the Reiki Master symbol, the subjects CDP trace is noticeably affected. I asked the Reiki master what making the master symbol meant. She told me that she draws the master's symbol in her third eye while simultaneously drawing it in the air with her finger. These are but a few samples of dozens of CDP traces

133

that I have collected; which indicate that some individuals do have the ability to somehow manipulate these bio-intrinsic or CDP energies using the volition of their minds. Some people can intentionally send energy across a room to affect the CDP traces of a test subject connected to the device. Like my grandfather and many others in tune with the universe, we all have the ability to do the same. We just have to believe it. I will explain how it can be done by almost anyone. I have already taught several people how to send the energy over distances and I will try to teach you later on in this book.

Before I get into the real interesting science stuff; I would like to tell you more about my personal life and how my interactions with the ET's has evolved and influenced my life since 1997.

Chapter 10
2001-2013
The Normal Life of an ET Experiencer

I am returning to my story in 2001 so I do not leave out the most important events of my life. It was the day I started dating a young lady named Holly. I cannot remember the exact date that Holly and I started dating. It was early 2001 when I started to get my life back together. Little did I know I was about to be set up. You see, my 11 year old daughter and Holly's 9 year old daughter conspired to get us together; and it worked. The relationship started with Holly getting my kids off to school in the morning while I went back to work and I would take care of her kids when they got out of school. Neither of us was looking for a relationship at the time, however, sometimes things just happen.

I did not want to scare her away, but I figured if she could not handle the truth; there was no point in pursuing a relationship. So, the first night we got together, I told her all about my U.F.O. experiences, my work with Lefty and some other crazy stuff; but she stuck around anyway. I knew if we were to be together that she would eventually be seeing things, so I wanted to prepare her. About two weeks into our relationship, I asked the ET's to let Holly see their craft flying somewhere near the house, so she would not think I was insane.

Later that evening we were heading west, out of town and we saw several metallic spheres hovering in the Western sky. We watched them for about a minute before they just disappeared. I believe this was one of the first times I asked them to show themselves to someone else. I was surprised, but not shocked, because I knew they had responded to other requests I have made of them. Holly took it really well. Since that time we have had numerous daytime sightings together. She has had several sightings on her own.

Holly and I were together for nine years before getting married. We started living together a few weeks after we met in 2001; but we wanted to make sure we could put up with each other before getting serious. I came into the relationship as a single father of four with sole custody of my youngest three children, two boys and a girl, ages 10, 11, and 12. Holly came into our relationship fresh out of a divorce with custody of her two daughters, ages 9 and 12. What were we thinking? I know what I was thinking. I was thinking; I finally found an intelligent, beautiful woman who accepted me for who I was. She was also crazy enough to get together with a guy that had four kids.

Honestly, Holly has been one of the greatest blessings in my life. If you have read the preceding pages, you know my life has not been easy. I have finally found someone to help me through struggles of day to day life in this reality. She is the strongest, most independent woman I have ever known.

Since we met, Holly has been the one constant which keeps my feet anchored to the ground when my head is up in the clouds. While my days are spent contemplating the universe, she is contemplating how we will be paying the bills. It is hard being an experiencer, but probably harder being married to one.

I have learned a great deal over the course of mine and Holly's relationship. There is however, one thing my wife has insisted upon since the day we met which seems to hold true in this reality and beyond: "The only one you can truly ever depend on is you." This does not mean that you can't ask for help and get it. It does not mean you are in this existence all alone. It does not mean we are not all connected. It means you need to take control of your destiny and determine your own future. You are the only one who can change your life. You must take responsibility and do what it takes to be who you want to be. I believe this holds true in all dimensions.

For the past thirteen years we have worked together to help each other raise seven kids in a blended family. Almost all of our children have had U.F.O. or paranormal experiences since we have been together. For our family, the paranormal is normal.

However; on the morning of December 4th, 2012, our normal life took an abnormal turn. Holly got out of bed to get ready for work; when she suddenly fell to her right, catching herself on the bed. At first she thought she had just gotten up too fast, but the balance issues continued. For the next three weeks her symptoms became worse; actually causing her to take almost a week off of work. By early January 2013, after numerous tests and specialists, the doctors still had not determined the cause for her symptoms. Holly does have a family history of major health issues and that caused us great concern. Feeling like I had run out of options; I asked for help.

I prayed like I usually do. I ask for God's love to guide me and the power of Christ and all good to protect me and mine. I asked for someone that was good to come and help my wife to be healed. I actually said, "Jesus, I really don't care who comes, as long as they are working with you." Now, you may be wondering why I did not try healing Holly. Well, I did pray for her, but when it comes to me doing direct energy work on my wife and the kids; that is a different story. It is like being the profit in your home town. To my wife, I'm just Phil; and to the kids, I'm just Dad. In order for energy healing to work, the recipient must be open to it; and be willing to be healed.

Knowing my wife as I do, I knew I needed help from a higher source, so I asked for it. Knowing that the ET's hear my thoughts when I project them to them; and no longer fearing them, I somewhat expected them to do something. But I did not expect to see them in the middle of the process.

Chapter 11
Is that an Alien
Hovering Over the Bed?

It was the first week of January 2013, Holly had been sick for almost a month and I was very concerned. That night I went to bed and prayed for someone to come and help Holly to be healed. At about 2:30 in the morning I awoke to see a creature hovering in mid-air, about 18 inches above my wife; whom was lying next to me in our queen sized bed. This being was two feet away from me or less. I looked at this thing and there was no fear. I did not scream like a little girl, or immediately reach for my .45, like I always imagined I would, if I had I ever saw one in my bedroom in the middle of the night. My response was nothing like I expected it would be; allow me to explain.

The following is a list of thoughts that ran through my head when I woke up and saw this being hovering over my wife. "Is that a grey? It doesn't look like a Grey. Its' skin is kind of greenish brown, not really grey. But it looks like a grey. It has the basic appearance of a grey; however it has a small pointy nose, thin, pouty, protruding lips, and a pointy chin. For some reason it's pouty lips and chin remind me of my wife's profile. This thing is floating in a supine position with its skinny little arms stretched out in front of it. I can only see the being from its head to its waist, because the rest of its body is still inside of the portal that is floating in mid-air at the foot of the bed. It looks to me like this thing is doing some type of intense energy work on my wife. Suddenly I realize that this being should not be there. The thoughts get the **** out of my room come into my head; but I speak only one word. At the top of my voice I screamed, "OUT!" This being looked at me like a deer caught in the headlights. Then it sucked itself back into the portal it was hanging out of; and was gone. Holly jumps up and says, "What the ***** is wrong with you?" I did not tell her what happened because I did not want her flipping out. So I blew it off as a bad dream. I told her I was just hallucinating. But it was no hallucination. There is one more unusual thing that happened right after the being left and Holly lied back down; I looked around the room and lied back down, and went back to sleep.

The following morning I told Holly what had happened. She did not know what to think; other than I am just crazy. When I started to think about what happened I remembered that I had asked for help. Then I started to feel bad for yelling at the being to make it leave. The more I thought about the situation the more frustrated I became.

I just wanted to know what the heck was going on. A couple of weeks after this event there were some U.F.O. sightings near Detroit. I was checking out the story online when I noticed that the guy they were interviewing; the current state director of Michigan MUFON, was Bill. Bill is an ET experiencer and friend I met fifteen years earlier. So I decided to try and get in touch with him to see if anyone had any real answers to the whole phenomenon. I really just needed to talk about it with someone that would kind of understand.

So I sent Bill an email and he got back to me the following day. The day after that, Bill received a call from a documentary film producer from the U.K. They were looking for contributors for a new UFO show. He said they were filming the show for a major U.S. cable network. Bill called me and asked me if I would be interested in talking to them; and I said yes. I never had a desire to go on a major cable television network and talk about my ET experiences. I did however want to tell the world about the CDP device. I thought that maybe I could get the producers to cover the CDP device on the show, or at least get them interested in the technology, If I did the show, so I decided to do it. The producers called me from London that same day and I told them a little bit of my story. A couple of months later; after talking about it with the family, they were filming at my home.

It took a couple of weeks of phone calls and Skype meetings with the producers in London before we began to work out the details of the filming. During our discussions I had the opportunity to pitch the possibility of discussing the CDP device in the film. The producers were interested in learning more; so I decided to set up a demonstration. I know several energy workers in Michigan, but none of them have the ability to control the energy like Edd. So I contacted Edd and he agreed to come up. He lives in the South, but was actually going to be working in Wisconsin just before the filming; so it worked out well.

I knew Edd had the ability to send energy to a person sitting across the room from him, causing noticeable changes in their CDP Trace; which is recorded using the CDP device. Basically we can use the CDP device to show that certain people can use the intent of their mind and the power of their brain to send bio-intrinsic or subtle energy across a room or across a country; from themselves to someone else. I honestly believe the world needs to know about the CDP device and what it can demonstrate.

Chapter 12
Observing Edd's Technique

The day before the filming, Jason, one of the producers from the U.K., came to my home to meet me and check out our home for the filming. So I set up a meeting between Jason and Edd for that same day. I had never met Edd in person, but I had spoken with him on the phone and heard many things about him from Lefty. However; I never saw Edd in action. What an experience. Jason showed up to my home a few minutes before Edd. After a quick introduction and some brief chit chat; Edd went right to work demonstrating his abilities on Jason. Pay attention here.

Edd had Jason stand up about ten feet away from him. He had Jason put his arms down by his side with his palms facing forward. Then Edd said, "Okay, you're gonna start feeling it." Edd is just standing there facing Jason. Suddenly Jason starts giggling; and says, "WOW," I feel it pulling me toward you." Then Edd says, "Okay, now I'm gonna push ya back a bit." Jason starts leaning backward and laughing. "What are you doing?" Jason says. I stood there in amazement. Edd was physically moving Jason from across the room, using his brain and his mind. I will explain later.

Allow me to explain to you what Edd calls his, "Gravity Wave." Edd can stand up in front of a crowd of people and perform his "Gravity Wave," and make the audience move in the following order:

- First; Edd says, "I'm gonna light up the back of my brain and pull ya to me," and then he pulls the crowd toward him.

- Second; he says, "I'm gonna light up the front of my brain and push ya back a bit" then he pushes them away from him.

- Third; he says, "I'm gonna light up my right side and pull ya to the left," then he pulls the crowd to their left.

- Fourth; he says, "now I'll light up my left side

and pull to the right," then he pulls the crowd to their right.

Edd can do much more than this process, but I consider this his basic warm up moves. While Edd was at my home for the filming, I saw him conducting his "Gravity Wave" on at least 15 people. Almost every time he would do it the same way and say the same things.

The day after Jason and I met Edd; the film crew and the cast arrived at my home to start shooting. Working with a real film crew and filming an episode of a new series coming to a major U.S. cable network was an awesome experience. However; I must say the most awesome thing about the entire experience for me, was what I learned from watching Edd conducting his "Gravity Wave". Allow me to explain.

The film crew was shooting at my home for an entire Saturday. We were scheduled to finish filming the episode, the following Wednesday and Thursday

149

in Grand Haven, Michigan. The day after the filming at my home, I was in my gym doing my tai chi; when it came to me. I figured out how Edd did the "Gravity Wave." At least, I thought I did. It was not until the following Thursday night that I was sure.

While we were at the motel in Grand Haven, I met a young lady in the lobby that knew one of the cast members in the show. We started talking and I started to tell her about Edd and what he could do; "the gravity wave." As I started to tell her about the gravity wave; I decided to try and show her instead. Sure enough, I started lighting up the back of my brain and she started giggling. When I light up the left side of my brain, it knocked into the wall. Wow. I freaking figured it out. Yes I am going to tell you how it is done. Just hold on. It gets better.

While Edd was at my home for the filming, he told me something very interesting about the energy. Edd said that he has done radio shows where he sends out the energy while he is on air and anyone listening can feel it. This is not a big surprise; however, he also said that people can feel the energy even when they listen to a recording of a previously aired radio show. This gave me an idea. I figured that if the energy can be felt from an audio recording; it should be felt from a video recording. So I made a video of me doing the "gravity wave" and a little more, and it works. When people watch the video they feel the energy and are physically moved by it. I even uploaded a couple of videos to You Tube. They work over You Tube.

The following is a brief description of an experiment I conducted on July 17, 2013 at Montcalm Community College in Sidney, Michigan. An old instructor of mine that is a PhD. Biologist, allowed me to conduct the experiment with the students from her Anatomy and Physiology class. The students were all female students that were enrolled in the Nursing program at MCC. Their ages ranged from approximately 18-40. All of them were aware they were involved in a blind experiment.

Intent of Experiment: To observe and record the effects of bio-intrinsic energies on human subjects that are observing a DVD that is "somehow" emitting bio intrinsic energies from a computer screen.

I began the experiment with a brief introduction of myself and my work in bio-intrinsic energy. I also gave a ten minute introduction to energy/quantum healing. I then informed the class that I had developed a device/methodology capable of imprinting energies on to a DVD that are emitted and felt by the viewer when being watched on any viewing screen. I then asked the students to stand in front of the large projection screen that was at the front of the auditorium. I had all of the students "open their energy meridians." I did this by having them stand up with their feet a little less than shoulder width apart. Next, they put their hands close together in front of their belly, their fingers relaxed and slightly separated. Many of them felt a very subtle magnetic energy field flowing between their hands. I had them slowly and gently move their hands in and out 1-4 inches apart, as if they were squeezing and stretching a small ball of plasma energy. As they moved their hands back and forth; I had them close their eyes and observe the motion of energy fields behind their eyes. I told them when they felt this energy working they should be ready to connect with the bio magnetic energy emitting from the large projection screen. I then had them place their hands down by their sides with their palms facing forward. Finally, I had the instructor start my energy DVD. Within 30 seconds the students were feeling the energy. The DVD shows only a black screen and has no audio.

The overall results were astounding. I believe every student felt the energy to some degree. Some students felt only a slight tingle in the palms of their hands. Others were moved back and forth to the point of stumbling. One student almost had a panic attack from the intensity. This particular student was so affected she had to step away from in front of the video screen within the first 60 seconds. After the video stopped, this student said, before the video, she did not believe in bio-intrinsic energies and thought I was crazy. She was visibly more affected than all the other students.

How is this possible? How can I use the intent of my mind and the power of my brain to imprint energies on to a DVD or digital media device? How is it possible that people can feel the energy being emitted from the screen they are viewing the video on? What in the heck is going on here? I think it has something to do with quantum entanglement. Allow me to try and explain to you how I see things.

Chapter 13
What I Currently Think About Our Reality

Everything is energy in its many forms and frequencies. Energy can never be destroyed; it can only change form. In fact everything that exists in the material universe is nothing more than energy consciousness applied to sacred geometric shapes and sacred geometric shapes with energy consciousness applied to them. Everything is energy on its many forms. If you have no idea what I mean, that is ok. I will try to paint a bigger more detailed picture for you; starting at the quantum level.

One day I went to Lefty's Lab; to help him with some research. The night before I went there I watched a remake of the movie "The Invisible Man." I show up to Lefty's and the first question he asks me is this; "Have you ever wondered how to make something invisible?" I said, "Of course." He said,

"In order to make an object invisible you need to change the spin rate of the atoms of that object." If you change the speed or frequency at which the atoms of an object vibrate, the spin rate, that object would no longer vibrate at a frequency that we could see.

Here is an example of what happens when we change the spin rate of the atoms of a coffee cup, for example. Imagine our coffee cup for a moment. It appears to be a solid object sitting motionless in front of you. But, on the quantum level, we know it is not.

The quantum particles which make up the atoms which make up the coffee cup are 'spinning' within a specific rate of speeds or vibrating within a specific range of frequencies. So the cup is not motionless. In fact, nothing is motionless. Every molecule in our universe is spinning within a certain range of speed; for discussion sake we will say "all molecules in our universe spin between 10 and 100 mph." It is because we are humans living in this universe we can only see things that are spinning between 10 and 100 mph. So if we speed up the molecules that make up our coffee cup to 101 mph or if we slow them down to 9 mph; we can no longer see the molecules that make up our coffee cup; so it disappears. It is invisible.

Here is a something more to think about. Human being can only see within a very specific portion of the light spectrum, ROYGBIV, the light spectrum goes far beyond human conception in both the infrared and ultraviolet spectrums; from radio waves to gamma rays. In the coffee cup example I just gave you; anything spinning at 9 mph or less cannot be seen, let's call this the infrared. The particles that are spinning at 101 mph or higher would be considered the ultraviolet. Now consider this, even though we cannot see the infrared or ultraviolet spectrums; they still exist. The same holds true for the coffee cup; we cannot see it, but it still exists.

What do I hope you get from this? I want you to understand that even though we cannot see something, it may still exist. I think this is especially true when it comes to understanding the existence of multiple dimensions. For now I want to discuss a little quantum physics and quantum mechanics.

Everyone should have the basic understanding that everything in the world, no matter how big or small, is made up of tiny particles; atoms and the things they are made of which are even smaller, protons, neutrons, electrons, quarks, leptons, and so forth. The study of these tiny particles is called Quantum Physics and or Particle Physics. These tiny particles and their tinier parts act differently in their super microscopic world, than things here in the big world. The Study of how these tiniest of particles behave as they interact with each other is called Quantum Mechanics. So when I say "Nothing is Solid," what I mean is, at this tiniest, quantum level of physical reality, there is empty space within the tiniest parts of the tiniest particles. Nothing is solid; we just can't see the empty space between these tiny particles which make up everything in the physical world.

We have already discussed how nothing is motionless; because everything in our universe is vibrating within a specific range of frequencies. Scientists call this vibrational state, Spin. But that is kind of a misleading word to describe the action.

Most of the matter we see around us is composed of protons and neutrons. Protons and neutrons are composed of a couple of different types of Quarks and Leptons. Everything from galaxies to mountains to molecules is made from this small selection of quarks and leptons; which are some of the smallest particles scientists have identified to date. But that is not the whole story. Quarks behave differently than leptons, and for each kind of matter particle there is a corresponding antimatter particle. There are four main interactions; attractive and repulsive forces, decay, and annihilation. These four things make the quarks and leptons change form, but they do not tell them what to change into. That is the job of the God Particle; the Higgs Boson.

There is a lot to know about quarks and leptons and how certain force interactions work together to create and decay all matter. I am not going that deep in this book. I will not go into detail on this subject either. But remember, the universe exists because these fundamental particles interact with each other. These interactions cause the changes in quantum particles which allow them to become matter. So in a real way, quantum mechanics puts and holds the universe of quantum particles together. But the God Particle tells particles what they should become. Now I want you to think about the possibility of other dimensions of space time.

String Theory

Allow me to present this as simply as possible.

String theory refers to the belief that we could potentially be surrounded by invisible or "untouchable" universes that are simultaneously existing at a different frequency or wavelength, just beyond the range of our ability to notice them. The reason it is called "string theory" is in accordance to it being likened to a vibrating guitar string. The more you tighten the string the higher the sound, the faster the vibration. When tension on the string is loosened, the string vibrates more slowly. The other universes are just a few notes off. The quantum particles of the other universes are spinning at a different speed than the quantum particles of our universe; therefore, they also have a different wave form. Some scientists theorize there could be eleven or many more alternate dimensions. I think the number could be limitless.

Think back to our coffee cup. We know it is just quantum particles spinning at a specific rate under specific quantum mechanical laws that apply to our universe. It is really nothing more than energy.

It could seem logical to conclude that other universes do exist just beyond our quantum speed limit and are operating under slightly different quantum mechanics. This concept helps me explain the being hovering out of a portal at the foot of my bed.

Quantum Entanglement

I wanted to present a brief description of quantum entanglement so that you are aware of the concept. When two sub atomic particles interact they can become entangled; meaning they somehow become linked and share some common properties such as spin or position. This is quantum entanglement. When scientists make measurements of one of the particles; this instantaneously determines the behavior of the other particle. Changing one particle, instantly changes the partner particle no matter how far the distance between the two particles. Einstein referred to this as, "spooky action at a distance."

I believe that scientists have proven that our consciousness can change the form that matter takes. This was accomplished by Youngs', 'interference experiment' or what is commonly known as 'the double slit experiment'. This experiment proved some very important things. First, it showed that one sub-atomic particle can be in two places at one time and can take the form of either a particle or a wave. Second, when scientists observed the particles during the experiment; it affected the results. When the sub-atomic particle was not observed it acted as a wave; occupying two places in space at one time. When scientists observed the experiment; the sub-atomic particle did not change into a wave; but remained a particle. They also discovered that the particles could travel back in time to change the results of the experiment. Current science cannot fully explain why this happens.

Chapter 14
Some of my Thoughts on Energy Healing

Some cultures believe you have a spiritual or energy 'Chakra' system, which consists of seven energy source centers which are part of your etheric body within you. Chinese medicine and Qi Gong are based on the proper qi flow. It suggests that humans have an internal energy system which consists of qi channels or meridians which carry qi throughout our bodies. This system also includes three main energy centers called the three, Dan Tian. Many believe that, through physical or mental dedication, through meditation, prayer, Yoga, Tai Chi, Qi gong, or martial arts, or other training, certain people can improve these energy flow system to improve their physical, mental, and spiritual lives. There is scientific evidence proving the existence of these energy centers. The CDP device is only one method.

I believe that energy healing is all about

healing the energy body; because the energy body is all that we really are. You see, if you heal the energy body the physical body will be healed. But what is the energy body? I believe the energy body consists of a combination of seven to twelve Chakras, three Dan Tian energy centers, and a complex system of energy flow channels or meridians that run throughout the physical body. The energy body is the embryo of your soul, and the physical body is a manifestation of the energy body. So if you heal the mind and the soul, the body will follow.

Before we try and understand healing we need to understand something about disease. All disease is caused from dis-ease. Disturbances in your consciousness, cause disturbances in the flow of bio-intrinsic or subtle energies through your energy body; causing problems to manifest in the physical body. When people fail to alleviate the dis-ease in their mind, they manifest disease in the physical body. So how is it possible for energy workers help to heal some ones disease?

Well it has been my experience that a few things have to be in order for energy healing to help eliminate someone's disease. First, the energy worker, and the person with the disease must truly want the disease to go away; the patient must be open to the healing. Second, it helps when the energy worker and the patient understand and believe in the effectiveness of the energy healing method.

Here are some more things a healing practitioner or energy worker should keep in mind:

1. Do all healing out of love and compassion, sending the energy so that it serves the most good for the individual receiving the energy. Remember these energies flow through your body from the universe; they do not necessarily originate within your body.

2. You're not God. You do not know the destiny of the individual needing healing so do not be disappointed if you do not see the results you

were hoping for. Someone may be dying of cancer because they chose that destiny. If you were to heal them you may interfere with their destiny or the destiny of their loved ones. Send the energy with the intention to do the most good. The real healing may need to take place in the hearts or minds of the dying persons loved ones. The energy knows where to go and what to do. The human mind is a powerful thing.

3. Find your own method of utilizing the energy. Whether it is prayer, Reiki, Qi-gong, Tai chi, or just faith, it is your journey, it is your choice. Personally, I go right to the source. I will describe a simple energy sending technique to you shortly.

4. Remember if you want to be a good energy worker, or just be a good person. My best advice to you is; Take a little advice from what Jesus supposedly said in:

Galatians 5:22.

"Live by the fruit of the spirit:
Love, Joy, Peace, Patients, Kindness, Goodness,
Faithfulness, Gentleness, and Self Control;
Above Such Things There is No Law"

Let me put it more simply:
Do the Right Thing!
Don't be a Jerk!

There are just a few more things I need to say about energy healing. Don't be silly about your physical health. Eat right, exercise, get your rest and think right. Go to a doctor if you need to. Use energy healing as a complimentary tool to smart health care. My suggestion is to stay healthy by thinking right and doing energy work daily. You are what you think.

Chapter 15
Angels, ET's, Inter-Dimensional Beings? Or All of the Above?

Before I discuss "them;" I want to talk about us. Who are we? Where do we come from? What are we doing here? Let me explain my view.

Who are we? We are all inter-dimensional energy beings. We are individual conscious minds that are innately connected through "Source Energy" to a Collective Conscious Mind. We can look at this Source Energy and the Collective Conscious Mind, as pieces of God the Total. We are also small pieces of God the Total. For God in His Totality; Is all things. Who are we? We are all pieces of God.

Where do we come from? We come from God, of course. However; how we came into existence from God is a very long story. I believe that our universe was created through the Mind Force Energy of Christ. By using his minds energy and sacred geometry; he caused molecules to form from the available God

Source Energy. I think the universe and planet evolved for billions of years. I think life was planted on the planet millions of years ago. I think humans evolved but were genetically manipulated at some point in time; probably around 400,000 years ago. We evolved and were genetically enhanced here. We come from Earth.

Why are we here? I believe we are here as ascending children of God. We are here to learn and develop our energy bodies; to increase our vibrational energy form and develop our universal minds. We are here to experience and grow. That is why we are here?

So are they angels, aliens, inter-dimensional beings, or all of the above? I say all of the above. I have to refer to the Urantia Book here because it mentions something called "Morantia Worlds." To the best of my understanding, Morantia Worlds are other dimensions that we can go to when we leave here. There are hundreds of Morantia Worlds, maybe

170

more. Jesus said, "In my Father's mansion, there are many rooms." I think if he were here today he would be able to say, "In my Father's universe, there are many dimensions." Well, my research into the topic leads me to believe that multiple dimensions do exist; even if we can't see them. Plus, I saw the front half of a being hanging out of a black hole, hovering in mid-air; the rest of its body had to be in another dimension. Yes, some of them must be inter-dimensional.

Are they Extraterrestrial? They have to live somewhere, don't they? I believe they are from other planets; however, those planets may be in another dimension. I think it is very probable that some of them could be from our universe; even our galaxy. I know they have craft that can speed off at incredible speeds or just disappear; so they have technology beyond our understanding. I am certain that most of them have a better understanding of reality than we do. I am sure they have the faster than light travel thing figured out.

Are they Angels? What is an Angel? I believe there are several types or orders of Angels. I guess I consider Angels to be energy beings that look over and assist mankind on behalf of "God". I believe Angels come from another dimension; a dimension closer to God Frequency. I do not know that I have ever seen an angel; but I saw some kind of being hovering over my wife. Was it an angel?

Here is the only angel related story I have. Back in 2002 I was visiting with my friend Suzanne at her health food store, discussing my recent work with Dr. Levengood. An elderly lady named Dorothy, whom I had never met, was standing near Suzanne. She was halfway involved in our energetic conversation and stated that she had practiced Therapeutic touch, when she was a registered nurse, during the 1970's. She explained how they were taught to envision a ball of light energy, the size of a baseball, between their hands before they began the therapeutic touch

172

session.

I jokingly replied. "I imagine a ball of energy, THIS BIG, and a spread out my arms as far as I could. Dorothy was at least twelve feet across the store from me when I made the motion with my arms. The instant I raised my arms I felt the energy fly out and Dorothy almost fell to her knees. Dorothy said I beamed her with a wave of energy. It didn't hurt, but was overwhelming. One thing is certain, this caught her attention. We made plans to meet and discuss therapeutic touch; I was hoping she could help me develop my healing abilities.

A few days later we met at her home. When she opened the door a giant smile came over her face. She welcomed me in and we began to talk. I said I believed in the Chinese proverb that says; "When the student is ready, the master will appear," meaning, I was there to learn from her. She laughed and said, "Oh, Honey you got that wrong, you are way beyond therapeutic touch." She went on to explain that when she opened her front door to welcome me in to her home, she saw that I was surrounded by a legion of Angels. The funny thing is it did not surprise me that much. So do I believe in Angels? Yep. Are Angels Aliens? Nope. Are Angels Inter-dimensional beings? Yes.

My Thoughts on the ET's Craft

There are some things I would like to discuss regarding the numerous crafts I have seen over the years, and how some of them maneuvered. My day time sightings include, saucer shaped crafts, triangular shaped crafts, walnut shaped crafts, cigar shaped crafts, Huge Blimp Shaped mother ship, small cylindrical craft, and small round craft. Many of the day time sightings I have happen when others are with me, they see them as well. I have had many sightings of lights at night; but I won't waste time discussing the insignificant sightings.

I would like to discuss the maneuvering I have saw some of these crafts perform. Many of the crafts I saw have had the ability to hover silently, some very stable, others very wobbly. Some appear to be very dark and solid, while others shimmer brightly. I have saw many of them accelerate at unimaginable speeds, while making 90 degree turns and vanishing off in the distance. However, many times the crafts will be hovering appearing very solid and suddenly, they disappear. When they disappear I have often noticed they somewhat shimmer away in a waveform. They can appear the same way; out of nowhere.

One day I witnessed five small wedge shaped crafts flying very slowly in front of me; and then they all merged into one craft. This was a daytime sighting that lasted for at least three minutes. The craft were approximately the size of a military fighter jet and were an estimated 50 feet in the air. I witnessed the craft fly just above a large stand of mature blue spruce trees. The trees were about 40 feet tall.

There is one incident in particular which is, to date, the best sighting I ever had at night. It was the one I referred to previously when the craft hovered directly over my head and suddenly took off, leaving a contrail of light. That is the best way for me to describe it. The ship was 30-40 feet above my head; when it sped off leaving a tube of light behind it that bent at nearly a 90 degree angle as it followed the craft off into space. How is the alien technology able to generate a photon trail, let alone, one that bends? Think about it. Bending light beams.

Here is something else I think; The ET's travel through space or inter-dimensionally at the speed of thought; by using their minds to connect with a form of source energy and somehow energetically and kinetically bond with their craft; moving their craft and themselves at the speed of thought to their destination. I think the so called "Roswell Metal" that Lefty had, could have been part of the control panel used to pilot the craft. I believe this, not only because of the shape of the largest piece of metal, but also because, even the small pieces of the metal we tested caused dramatic increases in a person's CDP energy reading. Meaning that the metal increases the amount of subtle energies we are generating. The metal also acted as a diode; meaning, it increased energy when used one direction and stopped the energy flow when used in the other.

Yes it sounds crazy, it is. Why me? Why do I see them so frequently? I know I am not alone, but I have met a lot of abductees and very few, if any, have as many sightings as I have. The abductees say it has something to do with my energy. People that have the ability to see auras look at me and often do not know what to make, Reiki masters, healers, psychics all sense an unusually strong energy from me.

My current thoughts on implants

I believe the implants are changing our physiology. Perhaps the implants are causing changes in our energy body which trigger changes to the physical body; changing our DNA. I think I asked for the one implant I have in my arm; to help me with my depression. I believe there are different implants for different reasons. I do believe some, if not all, of the implants are created from the compounds in our bodies. I do not think they are tracking devices. There is no need for that; we are all psychically connected. Please see the Afterword section of this book for some photos of abduction marks.

What I think about the pilots

I think some of them may be more consciously aware, more intelligent and technologically advanced. That does not mean they all have a set of moral values superior to ours. They can travel through space at the speed of thought. They can walk through solid objects and pop out of portals hanging in midair. That is all pretty impressive. They can also hear me when I direct my thoughts toward them. There have been multiple times that I asked them to reveal themselves to myself or others; and they would do so. At times they would show themselves instantly; other times I may have had to wait a day or so. I believe the ones I contact are here to help me. I don't know what to say about the others. I do know that one night on 2013, they healed my physical body; per my request. If you were to call it a miraculous healing, I would not disagree.

I do know that these beings have some incredible abilities; however, I believe we have abilities they do not. I believe it is related to our ability to use the power of thought and intent to tap in to these, bio-intrinsic, subtle energies, and direct them with our mind. Here in lies our greatest, virtually unused, ability as human beings. Technologically we may be retarded in comparison, probably evolutionarily as well, but do not give up hope. I am going to explain to you a small portion of what you are capable of doing with the power of your brain and the energies you can harness with your mind.

I know that some humans can levitate objects with the power of their minds. No need for an ankh or vibrating stone. You simple embrace the correct frequency and release the energies which are holding the object to the surface. I think humans are capably of walking through walls or walking on water; we just need to vibrate our energies to the correct frequencies. Where the energy body goes, the physical body will follow. I can't do these things yet, but I am trying to figure out how.

Chapter 16
Why are We so Special?

I believe we are special because we have the ability to change the material world with the power of our minds. We can do this individually or collectively. In fact; all that exists in our current reality is the result of our collective mass consciousness. Together, we literally create our own reality through constant interaction and action with the collective mass consciousness of source energy.

How can I prove that we have the ability to change the material world with the power of our minds? Allow me give you an illustration using energy work.

Let us say that a person with a cancerous tumor on their hand comes into an energy practitioner for a treatment. The energy practitioner performs their specific method on the client. At some point during the treatment the practitioner places their hands around the tumor; sending energy into the tumor; causing the patients affected hand to feel very warm. Let's say that the next day the tumor disappeared and left no traces of cancer. What happened to the tumor at the molecular or quantum level?

Here is what I think. The energy practitioner used the intent of their mind to channel the subtle energies from the universe into the patient's tumor. The subtle energies moved through the tumor and changed the molecular structure of the tumor. The subtle energies changed the particles of the tumor into something that was no longer cancer. So the practitioner used their mind to change the material world. What in the Higgs Boson?

Now let's take a more scientific approach as to how the tumor was changed. Remember, scientists know, that on the quantum level, everything in our material universe is made from quarks and leptons. But they do not know what force tells quarks and leptons what molecules to become. That is why scientists are in search of the God Particle; the Higgs Boson.

The following is my understanding and explanation of the Higgs Boson or God Particle; not to be mistaken for a real scientific definition."

The Higgs Boson or God Particle is the field of energy which determines which molecules that quarks and leptons should become; hence, the God Particle. Scientists at the large particle accelerators, such as CERN, are attempting to find the god particle; by recreating the BIG BANG, but in reverse. According to the Big Bang theory; all thing originated from one source of infinite energy and creative potential. All things are from one source; this leads to quantum entanglement.

What does this have to do with us? What happens when the subtle energies go through the tumor? It turns the cancerous tumor into something no longer a cancerous tumor. The subtle energies told the quarks and leptons in the tumor to become something else. So did the energy practitioner tap into the Higgs Boson or God Particle energy field and channel it through the cancerous tumor? Are these subtle energies part of the God Particle field? I see a connection. I think this is only one reason we are special.

Chapter 17
Neuropeptides and Energy Healing

I felt it was important to include this information about neuropeptides. The reason being is that I believe they are means with which the subtle energies connect with and influence changes in the physical body. I believe they travel the energy meridians of our bodies; and cause changes to the material body.

In the early 1970s, a neuroscientist and psychopharmacologist discovered the "neuropeptide" opiate receptor site on cells, which was to become one of many important advances in the scientific understanding of the mind-body connection. Neuropeptides are small, protein-like molecules that help neurons communicate with each other. They are found in the central nervous system, as well as in the peripheral nervous system. They act as messengers in the body, and perform specific functions. These molecules influence activities in the brain and body; such as food intake, learning and memory. They can turn on cellular function in the skin. Neuropeptides can also be pro-inflammatory or anti-inflammatory. An anti-inflammatory neuropeptide may be beneficial to the body as it reduces inflammation, increases collagen and elastin, repairs scars and wrinkles, and increases circulation. A person's mood, energy level, pain, pleasure, weight, cognitive reasoning, ability to form memories, and immune system regulation are tied to neuropeptides.

In his first book, Deepak Chopra, made the following compelling statement;

"The discovery of neuropeptides was so significant because it showed that the body is fluid enough to match the mind. Thanks to messenger molecules (neuropeptides), events that seem totally unconnected- such as a thought and a bodily reaction- are now seen to be consistent. The neuro-peptide isn't a thought but it moves with thought,

serving as a point of transformation. A neuropeptide springs into existence at the touch of a thought, but where does it spring from? (For example) A thought of fear and the neuro-chemical that is turns into are somehow connected in a hidden process, a transformation of non-matter into matter."

Chapter 18
Igniting and Directing the Energies

I have been researching and dabbling with subtle energy since I was a kid. When I was nineteen I found out my Grandfather Kava was a faith healer; and that furthered my curiosity in the field. For over 30 years I have been seeking better control of the subtle energies; I believe I have done it. Now that I have it, I must give credit where it is due; so thanks to Edd, whose dedication and hard work in the field of energy medicine, has helped me to find some of the answers I had been looking for. Thanks Edd.

Well, let me tell you how it happened. Edd came to my house for the filming of the T.V. show. While he was there I watched him give short distance energy treatments to, at least, a dozen people. Almost every time gave a treatment; he would say the same things. Before Edd started a treatment he would have the person receiving the energy stand about ten feet away and facing him; with their arms down by their sides and their palms facing forward. Then he would say something like this; "Alright, I'm gonna light up the back of my brain and pull you toward me." At this point the person usually starts giggling; because they should not be feeling what they are feeling. At that time the person starts leaning toward Edd. Next he says: "Now I'm gonna light up the front of my brain and push ya back a bit." They start leaning back. Then Edd says: "Now I'm gonna light up my right side and pull you to your left." They lean to the left. Finally Edd says: "Now I will light up my left side and pull you to the right." They lean to the right. It works.

I just told you how to do it. Or rather; Edd told you. It is that simple. You just, "Light Up Your Brain." I figured it out and I believe you can do it too. I have been playing with this stuff for years; so for me to have figured it out by watching Edd is pretty cool; but understandable. But there is something even cooler. I taught my nephew how to do it over the telephone. He has never studied energy healing; yet he was able learn the technique in less than ten minutes. Then I taught several other people, most of them had no background in energy work. I think they learned this technique so easily because the energies in the universe are changing. I believe we are in the midst of the great awakening. We are moving into the Age of Aquarius; a new era of light and life. I think that is why you will be able to learn this technique quickly. Are you ready?

Energy Balancing Technique

This is where I try to teach you the energy sending technique which appears to create similar affects to the technique which Edd conducted while visiting my home. This is my version of the technique; that I developed from observing Edd in action.

Before I get started I want to explain what you are going to do. You are going to be using all of your brain. You will be using your brain like a bio-electro magnet. During this technique you will need to think of your brain as being divided into four sections; Front, Back, Left and Right. In order to pull someone toward you, you light up the back section of your brain. To push someone away from you, you light up the front of your brain. To pull someone to their left, you light up the right side of your brain. To pull someone to the right, you light up the left side of your brain. Now find a willing subject to lock on to and give it a try.

Have them stand ten feet away from you with their hands by their sides and their palms facing forward. When you begin the procedure focus the energy through your subject. When you pull the subject toward you draw the energy from above and just behind your subject. When you push the energy toward them, draw the energy up from the earth, through you toward your subject.

1.   Stand up with your feet a little less than shoulder width apart.

2.	Place your hands in front of your belly and begin to move them; as if you were slowly clapping your hands; but do not allow your hands to touch. Keep them between one and six inches apart. As you slowly move your hands you should feel a subtle energy field flowing between your hands. It may feel like there are opposing magnetic fields in your palms. If you feel the energy, you are doing well.

3.	Now, close your eyes while you continue to slowly move your hands. You should experience some type of energy movement in your 3rd eye Chakra. You are igniting or "lighting up," your pineal gland, which is located between your eyes, in the middle of your brain. Most people feel the energies; some see light plasma or energy fields and others see cloudy waves of light. I feel an intense head band of energy right above my eyes; and see a ball of white light in my 3rd eye. When you notice the energy moving in your 3rd eye; your pineal gland is fired up; you should be ready for the next step.

4.   Now put your arms down by your sides with your palms facing forward.

5.   As you slowly breathe in, take the light form your pineal gland and begin to light up the back of your brain. To light it up, you take the energy field that you noticed in your 3rd eye; then move it to the back of your brain. You just imagine the light there and it will be; make it as bright as you can. When the back of your brain is light up you should feel the subtle energies entering your body from the universe. I feel a tingling sensation in my arms; it feels like it is pulling the energy from the universe into me. If you are locked on to someone they will start being pulled toward you. As long as you continue to light up the

back of your brain, you will continue to pull the person toward you. Remember to breathe comfortable during the process. You can knock people over if you pull too much.

6.   When you're ready, after a minute or so, take the light from the back of your brain and send the light to the front of your brain, lighting it up. I turn the energy into a small ball of light and lob it to the front of my brain. When you are lighting up the front of your brain you should feel the energy pushing out of your forehead. You may also feel the energy pushing forth from your heart chakra or the palms of your hands. When you light up the front of your brain the person you're locked onto should start to lean back away from you. As long as you continue to light up the front of your brain, you will continue pushing on your target.

7.   When you are ready, move the energy to either

the left or right side of your brain and light it up. Your target will lean in the direction opposite of the side of your brain you are lighting up. Be sure to move your subject in both directions. *"When I light up the left side of my brain I feel the energy being pulled into my left hand. When I light up the right side of my brain I feel the energy being pulled into my right hand."*

8. Now try to move your subject to the right by lighting up the left side of your brain. Just move the light to the left side of your brain and light it up. Hold the energy there for a minute or so.

9. Then move your subject to the left by lighting up the right side of your brain. Just move the light energy to the right side of your brain and light it up. Hold the energy there for a minute or so.

10. Finally, once you have finished lighting up the

right side of your brain for a minute or so; you should move the light energy to the center of your brain, back to the pineal gland, hold it in the center of your brain; centering yourself and your subject for a minute or so before you stop.

That is it. It is a simple technique that I believe anyone can learn if they sincerely wish to. Learning this technique is just the first step. There is much more to be known about working with these energies; far too much to discuss now. However, there is a great deal that you can do by using this technique. Remember that the energies you are directing will balance and heal the energy bodies of those receiving them. You see; if you can move someone from ten feet away; or from across the planet; you can also help them be healed from ten feet away or from across the planet. I have used this technique to move people from across the state of Michigan while talking to them over the phone.

In April of 2013 I stood in front of a video camera and conducted the technique. My intent while conducting this technique for the video was as follows: I intended for all that viewed the video to feel the energy and be physically moved; opening their minds to the reality that we are all connected through energy.

When people watch the video, they feel the energy and are moved. I uploaded the videos to You Tube and the videos can physically move people that view them over the internet. I think this is some really solid evidence for quantum entanglement; proof that we are all connected over time and space through the unseen energy source, from which all things began. This source is the source of the collective consciousness and of individual minds; the source of all creation.

There is something very important to consider when you send the energies and that is; your intent.

There is a way to send feelings and thoughts to other people by modifying this technique. Be conscious of your intent while utilizing this energy sending technique. You are far more powerful than you may realize. Remember KARMA? I am trying to avoid it. Please be nice and use this technique with Love. Thanks.

Chapter 19
The Great Conscious Awakening is Here!

What is the Great Conscious Awakening? I think I just explained it to you in this book. If you understood it; you are awakened. It is my opinion that the Great Conscious Awakening means that humanity is going to be awakened to a new understanding of conscious reality. I believe it is the reality I just described in this book; or something very similar.

Humanity needs to awaken to the reality that we are all multidimensional spiritual energy beings. We are all entangled on the quantum level, by subtle energy fields; because all things originated from One Source. We are all responsible for creating our shared reality, because we are all connected to source and mass consciousness. We are in control of our shared reality. Everything exists as it is in this reality, because we all agree it should be this way. We can change our destiny and make our reality anything we can imagine. There is an energetic change occurring in our universe that has begun to help this awakening occur. I just hope humanity will wake up real soon; because I think something catastrophic is coming.

The Birthing Pains

I think there is a real probability that we are about to see multiple ancient prophecies unfold on the planet; and they are not good. However; if we survive the birthing pains, we will help usher in the Golden Age. That is my hope for us all.

A few years ago, my boys and I spent the day with a biophysics researcher that had her lab personally funded by Lawrence Rockefeller. She told us that she was told that we do live in a binary star system and the government has known for years. They know that a major planetary cataclysm is coming and have been preparing for it for a long time. She said it was related to the planet Nibiru.

Nostradamus and other prophets have stated that we have the ability to change the future, and I agree. I do believe that, if enough of us could be awakened and come together, uniting our intent, we may be able to prevent these foreseen catastrophes. I do believe there is a possibility this could happen, but I feel the probability of this happening is very unlikely. There are too many arrogant, egotistical, ignorant and evil people on this planet. I believe the negativity and fear of their collective consciousness will bring some of these prophecies to fruition. It seems that only some type of catastrophic event will be able to fully remove the children of darkness and the damage they have caused, from the planet.

Prophets and remote viewers predict that the planet will be getting hit with a series of solar events that will scorch one third of the planet. Some prophecies suggest there will be a wave of photons that will come out of the galactic center and rake havoc upon the planet. I believe Edgar Cayce predicted a series of solar events or energy events that trigger a change in our genetic makeup; causing us to evolve into new beings in an instant.

The remote viewers have also predicted that ET or inter-dimensional beings will interact with mankind after the event occurs. However; most ancient prophecies and remote viewers have predicted the coming of a Golden Age, which will follow these cataclysmic events. Let's think this Golden Age into existence. We literally really can.

What concerns me most is what happens to us when these catastrophic events occur? Will we be in a safe zone? Will we have to hide underground? Will we be fried instantly? Will the ET's beam us up to safety? Will the energy of these events cause changes in our DNA that help us to survive the cataclysm and adapt to the new environment here? Or will the energies from these events trigger something within our energy bodies that enable some of us to shift into a new dimension of reality instantly?

Is it scientifically possible for us and the planet, to shift into a new dimension of existence; and what does that mean? I think it is possible for our current bodies and the planet to evolve into a new dimensional form; and I am not alone. I recently discovered the work of Nassim Haramein and I suggest you look into his theories. He does a great job explaining the science involved with some of the topics I discussed in this book. I am not a physicist, so I will try to explain it as I understand it.

I believe that the planet is going to get struck with a massive cloud of intense photonic energies; this may happen simultaneously with the massive solar events or may actually be the cause of the solar events. When this photonic energy field encompasses the planet, it is going to initiate a change in the spin rate of the molecules of our universe. Do you recall what happens when we change the spin rate, or speed limits, of the molecules of our universe? The material objects in our universe are no longer visible here; but they still exist they are just vibrating at different frequencies; in another dimension.

I want you to consider the following:

All matter in the universe is 99.9999 percent empty space. Within every particle in our universe there is empty space. Within every atom there is empty space. In fact, there is so much empty space within the molecules that make up the human body; if you were to remove all of the empty space from the molecules of every human being on the planet; the physical, solid matter, that remains would fit into a matchbox.

So how can our physical bodies shift into a new dimension? What Physical bodies? According to the above fact, all that physically exists of humanity could fit into three cubic inches or less. So if you take the content of three cubic inches and divide it by six or seven billion; that's how much physical body you need to change; A dust particle at best. Remember that we are just energy and energy cannot be destroyed; it can only change form. So how do we get that physical matter to change form? Remember who you are and what you can do with the power of your mind. You have the ability to harness and direct the subtle energies of the universe using the power of your mind. What happens to a cancerous tumor when the subtle energies are directed through it? It becomes something no longer cancerous; because force interaction and the subtle energies sent by the energy practitioner, worked together to cause the quarks and leptons to change form. The power of our minds can change matter.

Remember that all things are energy. We are energy. Energy cannot be destroyed it can only change form. We cannot be destroyed, we can only change form. The photon wave that is going to hit us is light energy. If God is light; are we about to get struck by the hand of God? Do you remember what Jesus said to the lady in Conyers Georgia; the place where I saw the Mother Mary statue smile. Will we return home with gold dust on our hands?

Will this prove to be the energy source we need to increase the frequencies of our energy bodies; turning on our dormant DNA and physically changing our physical bodies? Will this be the energy that raises our frequencies and the frequencies of the planet; shifting us into a higher dimension of reality? I think it is exactly that. I think and hope that we are about to evolve in the twinkling of an eye.

I am hoping that those of us that are having a conscious awakening will be able to shift into a higher dimension of existence; where we can create a new reality beyond our current comprehension. Help me usher in the Golden Age.

We are quantumly entangled, we are all continuously a part of the mass consciousness, with which we are literally creating the agreed upon reality we are currently experiencing. We can change the future. We do not need to experience the prophecies written in the book of Revelations. I am not buying into that reality and neither should you. I prefer to be one of those that just disappear; I don't want to be one of those left standing alone in a field. Do you?

"All matter originates and exists only by virtue of a force which brings the particle of an atom to vibration and holds this most minute solar system of the atom together. We must assume behind this force the existence of a conscious and intelligent mind. This mind is the matrix of all matter."

Max Planck

Afterword

U.F.O. Sketches

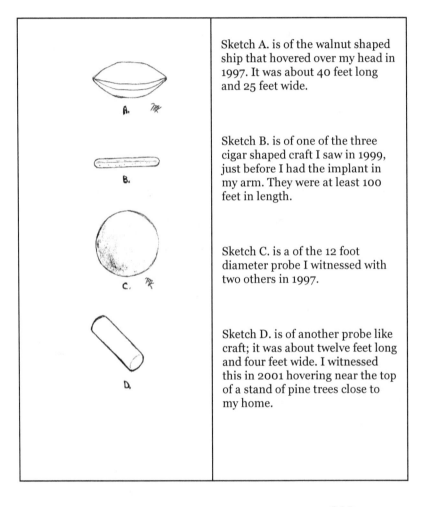

Sketch A. is of the walnut shaped ship that hovered over my head in 1997. It was about 40 feet long and 25 feet wide.

Sketch B. is of one of the three cigar shaped craft I saw in 1999, just before I had the implant in my arm. They were at least 100 feet in length.

Sketch C. is a of the 12 foot diameter probe I witnessed with two others in 1997.

Sketch D. is of another probe like craft; it was about twelve feet long and four feet wide. I witnessed this in 2001 hovering near the top of a stand of pine trees close to my home.

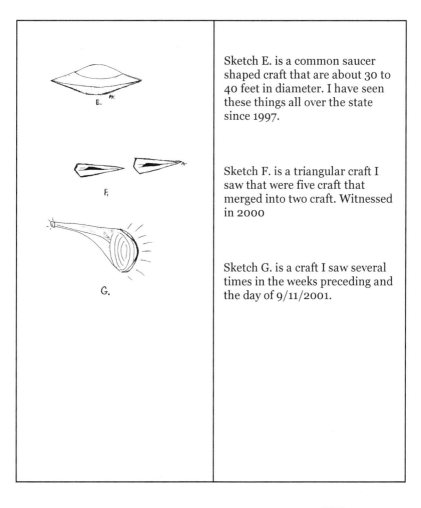

Sketch E. is a common saucer shaped craft that are about 30 to 40 feet in diameter. I have seen these things all over the state since 1997.

Sketch F. is a triangular craft I saw that were five craft that merged into two craft. Witnessed in 2000

Sketch G. is a craft I saw several times in the weeks preceding and the day of 9/11/2001.

209

Abduction Mark Photos'

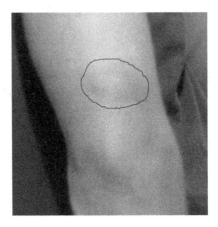

My right arm after 1999 sighting of 3 cigar shaped craft near my home. Black circle outlines the donut shaped bruise.

This is a tiny mark near my spine I received after asking them to show me they were responsible for it, 2/28/2000.

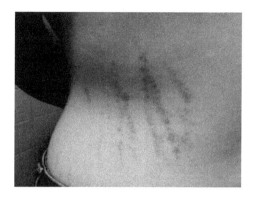

My wife woke up with these on her back
The same night I asked for and received a
miraculous healing of a serious health issue,
8/15/2013

CPSIA information can be obtained
at www.ICGtesting.com
Printed in the USA
LVHW080603060722
722857LV00014B/929

9 781494 790042